I Say, I Say, I Say

Brian Johnston was born in 1912. He joined the BBC's Outside Broadcasts Department immediately after the war and worked first on live radio broadcasts from theatres and music-halls all over Great Britain. He was one of the first broadcasters to work for both television and radio and began his long association with cricket commentary in the summer of 1946. Between 1948 and 1952 he also presented the live feature 'Let's Go Somewhere' for the popular Saturday night programme *In Town Tonight*.

He became the BBC's first Cricket Corres-pondent in 1963 and held this post until his retirement in 1972, after which he continued as a regular member of the *Test Match Special* team. He took over presenting *Down Your Way* from Franklin Engelmann in 1972 and continued for fifteen years.

He published two autobiographies and fourteen other books, including *Now Here's a Funny Thing*, *It's Been a Piece of Cake* and *Someone Who Was*. He died in January 1994.

Brian Johnston

I Say, I Say, I Say

*Johnners' choice of jokes
to keep you laughing*

with a preface by ROY HUDD

ARROW

by the same author

Let's Go Somewhere
Stumped for a Tale
The Wit of Cricket
All About Cricket
Armchair Cricket
It's Been a Lot of Fun
It's a Funny Game
Rain Stops Play
Brian Johnston's Guide to
 Cricket

Chatterboxes
Now Here's a Funny Thing
It's Been a Piece of Cake
Brian Johnston's Down Your Way
45 Summers
Someone Who Was

(with Peter Baxter)
Views from the Boundary
More Views from the Boundary

Reprinted in Arrow Books, 1998

1 3 5 7 9 10 8 6 4 2

First published in the United Kingdom in 1984 by Methuen
This edition first published in the United Kingdom by
Mandarin Paperbacks, and reprinted 6 times

Arrow Books
The Random House Group Limited,
20 Vauxhall Bridge Road, London, SW1V 2SA

Random House Australia (Pty) Limited
20 Alfred Street, Milsons Point, Sydney,
New South Wales 2061, Australia

Random House New Zealand Limited
18 Poland Road, Glenfield,
Auckland 10, New Zealand

Random House (Pty) Limited
Endulini, 5a Jubilee Road, Parktown 2193, South Africa

The Random House Group Limited Reg. No. 954009

www.randomhouse.co.uk

A CIP catalogue record for this book is available from the British Library

Papers used by Random House are natural,
recyclable products made from wood grown in
sustainable forests. The manufacturing processes conform to
the environmental regulations of the country of origin

Printed and bound in Norway by AIT Trondheim AS

ISBN 0 09 941689 1

Contents

Publisher's note

Brian Johnston's death in January 1994 left people all over the world feeling they had lost an old and beloved friend. Johnners was not only one of the greatest broadcasters of his generation but also one of the funniest and most popular *raconteurs* and after-dinner speakers. **I Say, I Say, I Say** is a collection of his favourite old jokes and anecdotes from all walks of life, including his beloved cricket, which Johnners had almost finished compiling before his death. Many of the jokes had appeared in his previous collection, **Now Here's a Funny Thing**, and in his preface to that book Johnners paid tribute to all those whose spontaneous wit and humour, and whose skill in honing a good joke to perfection (particularly the music hall comedians) had made him, and millions of others, laugh. He wrote: 'I have always enjoyed laughter. Either laughing at other people's jokes or stories, or trying to make them laugh at mine . . . All my life I have never been able to resist the chance of making a joke or pun.'

Preface

Brian Johnston was the Mirth Miser: he loved, cherished and
hoarded jokes. But, unlike Scrooge, he generously shared them
with whoever would give him a hearing. As you will soon dis-
cover, there is no such thing as a typical Johnston joke. They
range from schoolboy puns to complicated beginning, middle
and end shaggy-dog tales. They can be corny or clever, subtle
or sledgehammer obvious, rude or clean as a whistle. The only
criterion for inclusion in the Johnston Collection – they had to
have made *him* laugh.

Last summer, 1993, I realised a lifelong ambition, just. I
was Brian's very last interviewee in 'A View from the Boundary'
during *Test Match Special*. His opening line to me proved a great
start. 'Now Roy,' he said. 'You were born . . .' – a considerable
pause while he searched for my date of birth. 'Yes, Brian, I
was,' was my brilliant ad lib. The Johnners wheezy chuckle,
and from then on all downhill! As Brian could always do, he
skilfully turned the conversation to what he knew we had in
common. A love of music hall and variety. Within minutes the
jokes, word pictures and reminiscences flowed thick and fast
and the whole, totally self-indulgent, half hour finished with us
dueting to the only song he knew all the way through (or so he
said): Bud Flanagan's 'Underneath the Arches'. This, Gooch's
record-breaking innings, and our only victory over the Aussies
that summer, made it a day to remember.

But there was more. The interview done, Brian and I moved
back from the microphone and, *sotto voce*, carried on our chat at
the back of the commentary box. 'Right, Hudders,' said the great
man, 'let's have some new jokes now, please.' I happily regaled
him with most of the 'new' material from my stage act and left
him relishing the prospects of an English win.

That evening I did what I do for a living and afterwards, as is my wont, I was relaxing with a pint in the theatre bar. A gentleman approached me. 'I did enjoy the show,' he said. 'Thank you,' I wittily replied. 'But do you know, most of the jokes you told in your act Brian Johnston told on *Test Match Special* this afternoon?' The wicked old poacher must have done the lot during his next stint on the air.

I didn't mind – too much. At least my jokes were good enough for the master to nick – they'd made *him* laugh.

During his years of broadcasting he'd heard thousands of stories and laughed a lot. Everyone he met wanted to amuse him. He had an infectious chortle that made you forgive him even the unforgivable, laughing at his own jokes. And, joy of joys, you knew if you could come up with something that really tickled him you'd be rewarded with his unforgettable collapse into helpless gibbering jelly – just ask Jonathan Agnew.

Yes, Brian did hear the very best of jokes and he remembered the good ones. They're in this collection. If you recognise any of mine, please keep it quiet – I'm still doing 'em.

Roy Hudd

A

for Animals, birds and insects

A man went into a pub and said to the landlord, 'I've got a unique white mouse here. He can play the piano.'

The landlord roared with laughter. 'Come off it,' he said, 'pull the other one.'

'Well, I'll prove it to you,' said the man, and sat his white mouse down on the stool of the pub piano. It then proceeded to play a number of the classics and various tunes from musicals. The landlord was amazed and gave the man £50 for the mouse. Next day the same man came in with another white mouse.

'What does this one do?' asked the landlord suspiciously.

'Oh, this one can sing. If you don't believe me, ask the pianist mouse to play any song and this mouse will sing it.'

So the landlord asked for 'I Can't Give You Anything But Love', and the mouse sang it in a high treble.

'Remarkable,' said the landlord. 'My customers will love it. Here's another £50.'

The next day the man came in again. 'What have you got this time?' asked the landlord. 'Have you a mouse who can dance?'

'No,' said the man, 'I've got nothing today. It's merely that my conscience is pricking me. You know I said that the second mouse could sing? Well, it can't. The first mouse is a ventriloquist!'

Two fleas left a cinema. When they got outside one said to the other, 'Shall we walk or take a dog?'

Two fleas jumped out of Robinson Crusoe's hair. 'See you on Friday,' one shouted to the other.

A man sitting in the corner of a railway carriage kept tearing bits out of his newspaper, screwing them into small balls and then throwing them out of the window. The man sitting opposite asked him why he was doing it.

'To keep the elephants away.'

'But there aren't any elephants,' said the other passenger.

'I know. It's very effective, isn't it?'

'I call my dog Trueman.'

'Why?'

'Because he's got four short legs and his balls swing both ways.'

'I call mine Carpenter.'

'Why?'

'Because he's always doing odd jobs about the house. You should see him make a bolt for the door.'

'I've just had to shoot my dog.'

'Was he mad?'

'Well, he wasn't too pleased.'

'My dog's got the coldest nose in London.'

'How do you know that?'

'Whenever he comes into a room all the other dogs sit down.'

'Has your dog got a family tree?'

'No, he's not fussy. Any old tree will do.'

A man played the bugle and nearly got drowned the other day. He sounded the last post at a dog show.

A young girl wanted to give her puppy a drink. She asked if anyone had seen the dog bowl.

'No, I haven't,' replied her father, 'but I saw him make a brilliant catch on the lawn the other day.'

A fisherman saw a bowler hat floating on the river, moving slowly against the current.

'Are you all right?' he shouted.

A hand came out of the water and raised the bowler hat. A voice said, 'Yes, thank you. I'm on a horse.'

'Why are you looking so miserable?'

'I've just lost my dog.'

'Well, why not advertise for him in the paper?'

'It wouldn't do any good. He can't read.'

A whale was swimming in the Atlantic when he came across his friend the squid. 'How are you, Squid?' he asked.

'Not at all well. I'm feeling very ill.'

'All right, then, why not come for a ride on my back? I'm going to see my friend the octopus.'

So the squid jumped on the whale and after a short time they met the octopus.

'Hello, Whale, how are you?' he shouted.

'I'm fine, thanks,' said the whale. 'I've brought you that sick squid I owe you.'

Two flies in a teapot had a row. It all started when one flew off the handle.

Two lions were walking down the middle of Regent Street. One of them said, 'Not many people around today, are there?'

A farmer asked his young son to take a sow to the boar at the end of the village. On the way they met the vicar.
'Where are you going?' he asked the boy.
'I'm taking the sow to the boar, vicar.'
'Couldn't your father or brother do it, or can I help?'
'No, sorry, vicar. It has to be the boar.'

A blind man was walking along with his dog when it suddenly stopped and cocked its leg against the blind man's leg. He immediately felt in his pocket and, bringing out a biscuit, offered it to the dog. A passerby was amazed at what he saw.
'Considering what the dog has just done, that was a very kind act,' he told the blind man.
'No it wasn't,' said the blind man. 'I only did it to find out which end of the dog to kick.'

A vicar called on an old lady and much admired her talking parrot which he noticed had a red ribbon on its right leg and a blue on on its left.
'What are those for?' asked the vicar.
'If I pull the red one he sings 'Onward Christian Soldiers' and if I pull the blue one he sings 'Abide With Me', she replied.
'But what happens if you pull them both at the same time?' pressed the vicar.
'I fall off my perch, you silly bugger,' chipped in the parrot.

A woman had trained her parrot to give instructions to the various tradesmen when they called at the house. One day, when the coalman arrived, the parrot said, 'Ten sacks, please.'
When he had made the delivery the coalman said to the parrot: 'You're a clever bird being able to talk like that.'
'Yes,' said the parrot. 'I count too. Bring the other sack.'

A little old lady was sitting in front of the fire with her favourite tom cat on her knee. Suddenly there was a loud bang, a cloud of smoke, and a fairy appeared out of the fire.

'Little old lady,' she said. 'I can give you three wishes. What would you like?'

When she had recovered from the shock the little old lady said, 'First, I would like to be financially secure and live in a nice house for the rest of my life.'

The fairy waved her wand and the room was transformed into a luxurious drawing room, and on the table were sacks of gold. 'Next wish, please,' she said.

'Please make me young and beautiful,' said the little old lady, and she was immediately turned into a glamorous blonde. 'For my third wish, will you please turn my tom cat into a handsome young man?'

Immediately, standing before her was a fine specimen of manhood who stepped forward and took the lady's hand and kissed it, saying, 'Aren't you sorry now that you took me to the vet?'

A lady got on to a bus with a baby alligator in her arms. The conductor, somewhat surprised, asked: 'Are you taking him to the zoo, lady?'

'No,' she replied. 'We are going to the cinema. We went to the zoo yesterday.'

A man who lived next door to a pub had a favourite tabby cat. Unfortunately the cat was run over by a car and killed. A year later, at about midnight, the publican was doing his accounts. Suddenly the ghost of this cat appeared in front of him, holding half his tail in his hand.

'Can you help me, please?' said the cat's ghost. 'I expect you remember me when I lived next door. My old master has moved, so I thought I would try you.'

5

'Yes, I do remember you,' said the publican. 'You were a nice cat. What can I do for you?'

'Well,' said the cat's ghost. 'You see this bit of tail which I'm holding in my hand? It was cut off in my accident and I'm fed up carrying it around with me. Can you mend it for me, please?'

'I'm sorry,' said the publican, 'but much as I would like to, I can't help you. I'm not allowed to retail spirits after eleven o'clock.'

A crocodile went into a pub. The landlord said: 'Are you upset about something?'

'No,' said the crocodile.

'Well, why the long face?' asked the landlord.

A farmer was fed up with hikers going through his fields and disturbing his cows and the fierce-looking bull who was head of the herd. So he put the following notice on the gate into his field: *Admission free. The bull will charge you later.*

B

for Broadcasting gaffes

'There'll be an interlush by Ernest Lewd.' (Stewart Hibberd; Ernest Lush used to play an interlude between programmes.)

'Lady Diana's coach will draw up just below me here. She'll be met by her father, Earl Spencer, and they'll walk together up the steps into the Pavilion – er, I mean Cathedral.' (Brian Johnston outside St Paul's Cathedral on the Wedding Day of Prince Charles and Lady Diana)

'We're now going over for some chamber music in the bathroom at Pump.' (Stewart Hibberd; the Pump Room at Bath was regularly used for broadcasts.)

'If W.G. Grace was alive today, he'd turn in his grave.' (Anon.)

Lawrie McMenemy, interviewed on BBC after a Southampton defeat: 'It was our worst performance and our worst result. I blame myself. When you are 4–0 up, you should never lose 7–1.'

Rex Alston at Wimbledon: 'Louise Brough to serve, but there's a slight delay. She hasn't got any balls.'

'He was bowled by a ball which he should have left alone.' (Anon.)

'Botham has a chance of putting everything that's gone before behind him.' (Tony Cozier)

'West Indies have scored 244–7 all out.' (Frank Bough)

'His throw went absolutely nowhere near where it was going.' (Richie Benaud)

'The hallmark of a great captain is to win the toss at the right time.' (Richie Benaud)

'The slow-motion replay doesn't show how fast the ball really was.' (Richie Benaud)

Rex Alston was once doing a commentary at Lord's with E.W. Swanton as his summariser, to whom he referred for comment between the overs. The last ball of one over which he was describing got the edge of a batsman's bat and just dropped short of first slip who made a great effort to catch it. With his eyes still on the wicket, he said, 'Well, that was a very near thing for the batsman; though I don't really think we can call it a chance. However, it's the end of the over so let's ask Jim Swanton what he thought.' He turned round and, to his horror, found an empty seat beside him with the following notice written on a piece of paper – 'Gone to spend a penny. Back in a minute. Jim.'

John Snagge on radio, reading cricket scores: 'Yorkshire 232 all out, Hutton ill. I'm sorry, Hutton one hundred and eleven.'

'It's a catch he'd have caught 99 times out of 1000.' (Henry Blofeld)

'This is David Gower's hundredth Test. And I'll tell you something. He's reached his hundredth Test in fewer Tests than any other player.' (Don Mosey)

'That was a tremendous six. The ball was still in the air as it went over the boundary.' (Freddie Trueman)

'Anyone foolish enough to predict the outcome of this match is a fool.' (Freddie Trueman)

'Everyone is enjoying this except Vic Marks. And I think that he is enjoying himself.' (Don Mosey)

'Gatting and Lamb breathed life into a corpse which nearly expired.' (Trevor Bailey)

'The first time you face a googly you are going to be in trouble if you've never faced one before.' (Trevor Bailey)

'I don't think he expected it, and that's what caught him unawares.' (Trevor Bailey)

'That's what cricket is all about. Two batsmen pitting their wits against each other.' (Freddie Trueman)

'No captain with all the hindsight in the world can predict how a wicket is going to play.' (Trevor Bailey)

'On the boundary the small diminutive figure of Shoaib Mohammad, who can't be much taller or shorter than he is.' (Henry Blofeld)

'Welcome to Worcester where Barry Richards has just hit one of d'Oliveira's balls clean out of the ground.' (Brian Johnston)

'There's Neil Harvey standing at leg-slip with his legs wide apart waiting for a tickle.' (Brian Johnston)

'As you rejoin us at Leicester, captain Ray Illingworth has just relieved himself at the Pavilion End.' (Brian Johnston)

'The bowler's Holding, the batsman's Willey.' (Brian Johnston)

When asked if there was any chance of any play on the Saturday of a Test Match between England and India at Old Trafford:
　'No, I'm afraid not. It's wet, cold and miserable here, and I can see a dirty black crowd, er – I mean cloud.' (Brian Johnston)

'Play has ended here at Southampton but they are going on until seven o'clock up at Edgbaston. So over now for some more balls from Rex Alston.' (Brian Johnston)

'The Queen of Norway is wearing an off-the-hat face.' (Max Robertson)

'The Queen Mother is dressed in dark black.' (Audrey Russell)

'You've come to me too late. The Queen's just gone round the bend.' (Henry Riddell at the Opening of Parliament)

'The New Zealand team are now being presented to Her Majesty. It's a great occasion for these Commonwealth teams to meet the Queen. It's a moment they'll always forget.' (Robert Hudson)

At Lord's in 1969 Alan Ward bowling very fast from the Pavilion End hits Glen Turner a terrible blow in the box off the *fifth* ball of his over. Turner collapses in the crease, writhing in pain for about three minutes. He then staggers to his feet looking pale and obviously in great pain.

'Turner has now got up off the ground and, although looking pale and shaken, is obviously going to resume batting. A very brave effort. One ball left!' (Brian Johnston)

C

for Cricketers

When he was up at Oxford, Jon (Pom-Pom) Fellows-Smith used to have his leg pulled unmercifully by Jumbo Jowett. One day Pom-Pom was sitting writing letters in the dressing room in the Parks. This is at the back of the pavilion and is underground so that it is impossible to watch the game from it. Jumbo rushed in and said, 'You're in, Pom-Pom.' Pom-Pom picked up his batting gloves and bat and walked out, and as was usual with him, kept his eyes fixed on the ground with his bat trailing behind him. When he had got about halfway to the wicket he heard roars of laughter from the crowd. Looking up he saw that the game was going on in the middle and that no one was out. He returned to the pavilion threatening to 'fill Jumbo in'.

In the next match *v.* Middlesex, he was again writing letters in the dressing room when a young chap being tried for the University went in to bat. Pom-Pom was the next man in. After about two minutes Jumbo Jowett again rushed in and said, 'Lawrence is out, you're in, Pom-Pom,' but this time Pom-Pom refused to believe him and went on writing his letter. He wasn't going to be caught twice! However, a few moments later Lawrence came into the dressing room and began taking off his pads, so Pom-Pom realised that this time Jowett had *not* been pulling his leg. He picked up his batting gloves and again rushed out to the wicket. But still determined not to be caught out a second time he looked up as he walked, and to his surprise he saw that there was no one on the field except the two umpires. J.J. Warr, who was captaining the Middlesex team, had been let in on the joke and had taken all his team and hidden them behind the sightscreen!

What Pom-Pom said cannot be printed in this book!

Once when Middlesex had to follow on due to some very bad batting, one of the Middlesex batsmen in the dressing room called out to John Warr, 'What's the order in the second innings, Skipper?'

Warr replied, 'Same order – different batting.'

While in Australia with the 1962/63 MCC Team, the Rev. David Sheppard came in for more than his fair share of dropped catches. The story was going around that a young English couple who had settled in Australia were due to have their first-born christened. The husband suggested that it would be nice if they got David Sheppard to do it for them. 'Oh no,' said the horrified wife, 'not likely, he would only drop it!'

Yorkshire were playing Somerset in the good old days. Emmott Robinson was bowling when in came the next batsman: a real gentleman, I Zingari, bristling moustache, silk shirt ('Never wore a vest in my life!'), spotless batting trousers, well-whitened pads and boots, and a highly coloured fancy cap.

'Good morning, Robinson,' he said on his way to the wicket.

Emmott took an immediate dislike to him. The batsman arrived at the wicket, took guard, and then took ages looking round the field, walking or strutting around as he did so. At last the batsman was ready, and Emmott bowled him a snorter, pitching on the leg stump and hitting the top of the bail off. On his way out he said, 'Well bowled, Robinson, it was a fine ball.'

And Emmott replied, 'Aye, but t'were wasted on thee.'

On the day Fred Price made his record of seven catches in a County Championship innings, he was having a drink in the Tavern after the game, when a lady came up to him and said,

'Oh, Mr Price, I did admire your wicket-keeping today. I was so excited, I nearly fell off the balcony.'

'If you had done so, madam,' he replied, 'on today's form I would have caught you too!'

Before the start of a needle village match, the home captain found he was one short. In desperation he was looking round the ground for someone he could rope in to play when he spotted an old horse grazing quietly in the field next door. So he went up to him and asked if he would like to make up the side. The horse stopped eating and said, 'Well, I haven't played for some time and I'm a bit out of practice but if you're pushed, I'll certainly help you out.' And so saying, he jumped over the fence and sat down in a deckchair in front of the pavilion.

The visitors lost the toss and the home side batted first, the horse being put in last. They were soon 23 for 9 and the horse made his way to the wicket wearing those sort of leather shoes horses have on when they are pulling a roller or a mower. He soon showed his eye was well in and hit the bowling all over the field. When he wasn't hitting sixes he was galloping for quick singles and never once said 'Neigh' when his partner called him for a run. Finally he was out hoof before wicket for a brilliant 68, and the home side had made 99.

When the visitors batted the home captain put the horse in the deep and he saved many runs by galloping round the boundary and hoofing the ball back to the wicket-keeper. However, the visitors were not losing any wickets and were soon 50 for 0. The home captain had tried all his regular bowlers in vain when he suddenly thought of the horse. He had batted brilliantly and now was fielding better than anyone. At least he could do no worse than the other bowlers.

So he called out to him, 'Horse, would you like to take the next over at the vicarage end?'

The horse looked surprised. 'Of course I wouldn't,' he replied. 'Whoever heard of a *horse* who could *bowl*?'

It appears that when 'Bomber' Wells was playing for Gloucestershire he was batting one day with Sam Cook. They got into a terrible tangle over a short single, with Sam just making the crease by hurling himself flat on the ground. As he lay there panting he shouted to 'Bomber', 'Call!' – and 'Bomber' shouted back, 'Tails!'

In a Lancashire match a fast bowler was bowling on a bad wicket, and the opening batsman – who shall be nameless – had to face a number of terrifying deliveries. The first whizzed past his left ear – the second nearly knocked his cap off – and the third struck him an awful blow over the heart. He collapsed and lay on the ground, then, after a minute or two, got up and prepared to take strike again. The umpire asked him if he was ready. He replied, 'Yes, but I would like the sightscreen moved.'

'Certainly,' said the umpire. 'Where would you like it?'

The batsman replied, 'About halfway down the wicket between me and the bowler!'

In a village match a batsman came in with only one pad. Frank Woolley pointed out to him that he only had one, and the chap said, 'Yes, I know, but we only have five pads between us.'

'But,' said Frank, 'you've got it on the wrong leg.'

'Oh no,' said the batsman, 'I thought I would be batting at the other end!'

One day Emmott Robinson arrived at Old Trafford for the Roses Match. He was first there. He looked in the Lancashire dressing room. No one there. He looked back into the Yorkshire dressing room. There was still no one there, so he shut the door – locked it – and, taking off his trilby, knelt down and prayed as follows:

'Oh Lord above, Thou art the greatest judge of this game of cricket which is to take place today between those two great counties, Yorkshire and Lancashire. If Yorkshire are the best side they will win. If Lancashire are the best side they will win. If the two sides are equal or if it rains it will be a draw. But if Tha will just keep out of it for three days, we will knock Hell out of 'em!'

In a village cricket match a very fat batsman came in to bat, and as he was taking up his stance at the wicket the local umpire confided to the visiting bowler: 'We have a special rule for him. If you hit him in front it's lbw, if you hit him behind it's a wide!'

In one Leicestershire *v.* Nottinghamshire match H. Smith unwisely bowled some bumpers at Harold Larwood, much to the consternation of his own team, who realised what they would be in for when it was their turn to bat. However, he obstinately insisted on bowling short. When Leicestershire went in Larwood controlled himself very well against the early batsmen. It wasn't until Smith came in low in the order that Larwood really got down to business. He bowled a succession of terrifying bumpers, to one of which Smith got an edge which sent the ball first bounce into the hands of Sam Staples in the slips. Smith started to walk back to the pavilion, but Sam called out to him, 'All right, it wasn't a catch.'

'That's what you think,' said Smith. 'It's good enough for me,' and continued his walk back to the dressing room.

When coach at Harrow, Wilfred Rhodes was very insistent that his young charges should play all their strokes academically. One day one young fifteen-year-old, ignoring his mentor's instructions, thrust out his left foot, and took a mighty swing at the ball which went sailing through the air for a hundred yards or more.

'That's no good,' said Wilfred. 'Look where thar feet are.'

'Yes,' said the boy, 'but look where the ball is!'

The Church of England received a challenge from the Roman Catholics to a cricket match at Lord's. The Archbishop of Canterbury was naturally keen to know what sort of chance his side would have before he took up the challenge, so he conferred with the Rev. David Sheppard, who recommended acceptance only if the C of E could obtain the services of Ken Barrington. The Archbishop took his advice. He summoned Barrington, specially ordained him, and immediately accepted the challenge.

At half past one on the day of the match he rang up Lord's to ask David Sheppard the score.

'I'm sorry, Your Grace, but we are 44 for 9.'

'How dreadful! What happened to the Rev. Kenneth Barrington?'

'Out first ball, I'm afraid.'

'Who is doing all the damage, then?'

'A fellow they've got called Father Trueman!'

Leicestershire were playing Nottinghamshire and Harold Larwood was bowling at his fastest and was in his most frightening mood. The light was very bad and he had taken four quick wickets when it was Alex Skelding's turn to bat. He came down the pavilion steps very slowly, then groped his way along the railings in front of the pavilion, shouting to the members, 'Can anyone tell me where this match is being played . . . ?'

As a young nineteen-year-old, Alf Gover arrived at Lord's for his first Middlesex v. Surrey match. When he got to the 'old Pro's' dressing room, only one other person was there – the great Patsy Hendren. 'Hello, young chap,' he called out. 'What's your name?'

'Alf Gover, sir.'

'What do you do?'

'I bowl.'

'Quick?' said Patsy.

'Very quick,' he answered proudly. Patsy looked round the room to make sure that he was not overheard, came over to

17

him and said, very confidentially, 'Look, son, I don't mind quick bowling, you can push it down at me as fast as you like, only . . .' – another conspiratorial glance around – 'only I don't like 'em if they are pitched short. You know this is my home ground and they like me to get a few. My peepers aren't as good as they were and I can't pick up the ball as fast as I used to, so keep them well up to me, won't you?' Alf pondered on this self-admitted fear of the great England and Middlesex batsman and decided that there was a great chance for him to make his name.

Alf happened to be bowling from the Pavilion end when Patsy came in. He said to himself, 'Ah, here's that old man who can't see and doesn't like short-pitched balls – so here goes.' His first ball to him was very short, just outside leg stump and as fast as he could bowl it. It was promptly hooked for six into the Tavern.

'Fluke,' said Alf to himself and sent him down a similar short ball, only this time on the middle stump. Patsy took two steps back and cut it for four past third man.

'I've got him scared now – he's running away,' said Alf to himself as he walked back to his mark. Down came the third ball just the same as the other two and it went sailing away for six into the Mount Stand.

At the end of the over Jack Hobbs came across to him from cover. 'What are you bowling short at Mr Hendren for, son?'

'He's afraid of them,' he answered.

The 'Master' looked at him in amazement. 'Who told you that?' he asked.

'He did, Mr Hobbs,' said Alf.

Jack Hobbs raised his eyebrows. 'Don't you know he's the best hooker of fast bowling in the world? And what's more, young man, I'd remind you he's an Irishman and every night he kisses the Blarney Stone!'

And so Alf learnt to his cost – and Surrey's – that not only was Patsy Hendren one of England's greatest batsmen and one of the best hookers the world had ever known, but also its most superb leg-puller.

It was a Sunday in Australia, and Percy Chapman and Patsy Hendren decided to get away from it all and borrowed a car for a run into the country. After a few miles they went round a corner and saw a cricket match about to start in a field adjoining the road. As all cricketers are wont to do, they stopped the car with the intention of watching the game for a few minutes. The car no sooner stopped than an Australian strolled over to the car and said, 'Do either of you chaps play cricket?'

Chapman pointed to Patsy and said, 'He plays a little.'

'Good-oh,' said the fellow, 'we're a man short. Will you make up for us?'

Although it was Patsy's day off he obliged, and as his adopted side were fielding the captain sent him out to long-on. Patsy went to the allotted position, and as the field was on a slope he was out of sight of the pitch. He had nothing to do except throw the ball in occasionally. He was lost to sight for a long time when at last a towering hit was sent in his direction. Patsy caught the ball and ran up the hill, shouting, 'I caught it, I caught it!'

The batsman looked at him with daggers drawn – it was *his* captain. 'You lunatic! *They* were out twenty minutes ago. *We're* batting now!'

The food at a cricket club dinner was not up to standard. One of the members wrote to the secretary to complain.

'*I'm so sorry you didn't enjoy your meal*,' wrote back the secretary. '*Will you please bring it up at the annual general meeting?*'

In a match against Gloucestershire Brian Close was fielding at forward short leg with Freddie Trueman bowling. Martin Young received a short ball which he hit right in the middle of the bat. It hit Close on the right side of the head and rebounded to first slip who caught it!

Close seemed none the worse but when he returned to the pavilion at the next interval the Secretary of Gloucestershire, R.J.G. McCrudden, asked him, 'That was a terrible blow. Aren't you worried, standing so near? What would have happened if the ball had hit you slap between the eyes?'

'He'd have been caught at cover,' replied the indomitable Yorkshire captain!

Yorkshire were playing the South Africans at Sheffield, and the late H.B. Cameron went in to face the bowling of Hedley Verity. Cameron took guard and hit the first ball over the pavilion for six. The next three balls all went for four and the last two for six each, making 30 runs off the over. Verity passed Arthur Wood at the end of the over, with a face as long as a collie's, but Arthur said, 'You don't want to worry, Hedley, you've got him in two minds.'

'Two minds?' said Verity. 'What do you mean, two minds?'

'Oh,' said Arthur, 'he doesn't know whether to hit you for four or for six.'

During Peter May's tour of Australia in 1958–9 MCC suffered so many injuries that they had to send back for reinforcements. Ted Dexter and John Mortimore were flown out to join the team. Two elderly members of a well-known club in St James's Street were discussing the situation. One of them said to the other, 'I can see that MCC have had so many injuries that they're sending out some more players.'

'Yes,' said the other, 'I've just read that they're sending Mortimore.'

'*How* many?' exclaimed the first member. '*Forty* more! I didn't know it was as bad as that!'

In 1948 Alec Bedser and Jack Crapp arrived late at the Queen's Hotel on the night before the Test at Headingley. Alec asked Jack to take in their two suitcases while he parked the car round the back of the hotel.

Jack approached the reception desk where the receptionist,

thinking she was welcoming a new customer, said, 'Good evening. Bed, sir?'

'No, Crapp,' replied Jack.

'Second door on the left,' said the receptionist.

Alan Ward went to play cricket in Germany for a club side. He bowled very fast and took a hat-trick. He was promptly nicknamed Jerry Hat-trick Ward.

A cricketer who was asked what he was going to do during the winter months – and wanting to be in the current fashion – said, 'Oh, I shall write a book, of course.'

'Oh, said the questioner, 'what on?'

The cricketer, being fairly learned, said, 'On Ethics.'

'Oh,' said his friend, 'I thought you played for Sussex.'

George Gunn, when playing for Nottinghamshire against Glamorgan, started to walk off the field at half-past one under the impression that it was time for lunch. However, under the conditions for that match, lunch was not due to be taken until two o'clock and Gunn was recalled to continue his innings. He lifted his bat away from the next ball, was comprehensively bowled, making no attempt to play the ball, and as he retired to the pavilion, said, 'You can have your lunch, gentlemen, when you like, but I always take mine at one-thirty.'

D

for Doctors and dentists

A man went to see his doctor.

'I'm not well, doctor. There's something wrong with me. In the mornings I think I'm a wigwam, and in the afternoons I think I'm a marquee.'

The doctor examined him and said, 'I'm going to give you a sedative. You are *two tents*.'

A man told his doctor that he wasn't feeling at all well. The doctor asked him what he ate during a day.

'Well, doctor, at breakfast I have three billiard balls, two yellow, one blue. For lunch I have two brown, and a pink. For tea a yellow. For supper three blacks.'

'I'm not surprised you're not well, on that diet – you're not having enough greens.'

A man swallowed his watch, so the doctor gave him some pills to help pass the time away.

A young wife went to a dentist and said she had toothache, but that she was terrified of being hurt by him.

'I really am scared,' she said. 'I don't know which is worse – having a tooth stopped or having a baby.'

'Well,' said the handsome young dentist. 'Make up your mind before I adjust the chair!'

A woman went to a doctor with a bad cough. After he had examined her, he said. 'Do you ever get a tickle in the morning?'

'Well, I used to,' replied the woman, 'but not now. They've changed the milkman.'

A mother took her ten-year-old son to the doctor.

'Doctor,' she said. 'I'm very worried. My son thinks he's a hen, and can't stop clucking.'

'How long has this been going on?' asked the doctor.

'Oh, about five years,' replied the mother.

'Then why on earth didn't you bring him to me before this?'

'Well, candidly, doctor, we needed the eggs.'

A small boy swallowed a £5 note. His mother rang up the doctor in a panic.

'What shall I do, doctor?'

'Oh,' said the doctor, 'give him some pills and give me a ring in two days' time if there is no change.'

A nun visited a doctor with a violent attack of hiccups. The doctor told her she was pregnant.

After she had gone, his assistant asked him if she really was. 'No,' said the doctor. 'But the shock stopped her hiccups.'

A man was worried about his sex life.

'How often should I have sex, doctor?' he asked.

'Infrequently,' said the doctor.

'Is that one word or two?' asked the man.

An absent-minded man went to see a psychiatrist.

'My trouble is,' he said, 'that I keep forgetting things.'

'How long has this been going on?' asked the psychiatrist.

'How long has *what* been going on?' said the man.

23

A man went to the doctor's with very bad laryngitis. The receptionist, who was a lovely girl, opened the door.

'Is the doctor here?' he whispered hoarsely.

'No,' she replied in a whisper, 'come in.'

A man broke his finger which his doctor put into a splint.

'Will I be able to play the guitar when it's better?' he asked the doctor.

'Yes, of course you will,' the doctor replied.

'Funny,' said the man, 'I've never been able to play it before.'

An attractive young girl suddenly felt ill in the middle of the night. Her father rang the doctor and asked him to come as soon as possible. When the doctor arrived he rushed up the stairs and the father showed him into his daughter's bedroom. The father then went downstairs where he and his wife had a cup of tea. After about half an hour they wondered what was wrong with their daughter, so anxiously went and listened outside her bedroom door. Hearing voices, the father listened at the keyhole.

He heard his daughter pleading, 'Kiss me, doctor, kiss me.'

'I'm sorry, young lady, I can't do that,' replied the doctor. 'It would be completely unethical. Strictly speaking, I shouldn't even be in bed with you.'

A man with a bad inferiority complex went to see his doctor.

'Doctor, please help me. Nobody ever notices me.'

The doctor said, 'Next patient, please.'

Doctor: 'I'm afraid I can't diagnose your complaint. I think it must be drink.'

Patient: 'All right then, I'll come back when you're sober.'

A man went to see his doctor because his hands kept shaking.

'Do you drink much?' asked the doctor.

'No,' said the man. 'I spill most of it.'

A man went to see a doctor in great panic.

'Doctor, please examine me at once. I think I'm going to have a baby.'

The doctor examined him and said, 'By God, you're right. This will cause a tremendous sensation when I tell my colleagues in Harley Street.'

'It will back home in Laburnum Crescent too,' said the man. 'I'm not even married.'

'Doctor, doctor. My little Willie has just swallowed a teaspoon. Please come at once.'

'Very well, madam. I'll be right round. But meanwhile, tell him to sit still and not to stir.'

A doctor was visited by a patient who complained that he snored so loudly that he even kept himself awake.

'I suggest that you try sleeping in another room,' said the doctor unhelpfully.

Doctor: 'What's the matter with you?'

Patient: 'I keep thinking I'm a pack of cards.'

Doctor: 'Well, stop shuffling about and I'll deal with you in a minute.'

Patient: 'I keep thinking I'm a pair of curtains.'

Doctor: 'Come, come. Pull yourself together.'

A man went to the doctor's and complained that he thought he was an umpire.

Doctor: 'How's that?'

Man: 'Not out.'

A man went to his doctor and asked if he could recommend any form of male contraception.

'Yes,' said the doctor. 'Put a stone in your shoe. It will make you limp.'

A woman was sitting nervously in the dentist's chair waiting to have a tooth stopped. The dentist approached her with the drill and asked her to open her mouth.

Suddenly, he stopped and said, 'Excuse me, madam. Do you realise that your right hand is gripping me in a very painful place?'

'Yes,' said the woman, 'I do. We're not going to hurt each other, are we?'

E

for Education

There were two deadly rivals at school who hated each other. After they had left, their paths never crossed. One became an admiral, the other a bishop. One day there was an important function at Windsor Castle to which they had both been invited. It was a full ceremonial dress affair and they were both on the platform waiting for their train to Windsor. Both were in their full regalia, the admiral in his cocked hat, and the bishop, who had become very portly, in his black frock and gaiters.

The bishop suddenly recognised his old rival, so walked up to him and said, 'Excuse me, station master, what time does the train for Windsor leave?'

The admiral immediately spotted who it was and replied, 'At one o'clock, madam, but in your present advanced state I would recommend you not to travel.'

The class had been asked to write a short essay on 'The Pleasures of Childhood'. One little boy wrote: "The pleasures of childhood are great but not to be compared with the pleasures of adultery.'

A young boy arrived late at school.

'Why are you late, Johnny?' asked the teacher.

'I'm sorry, miss, but I had to get my own breakfast today.'

'All right, Johnny. Settle down. We are doing geography and

here is a map of India and Pakistan. Can you tell me where the Pakistan border is?'

'Yes, teacher, in bed with Mum. That's why I had to get my own breakfast.'

An ancient and rather doddery headmaster prided himself on his memory and always boasted that he could remember anyone's name. At an old boys' gathering he went up to one of them and said, 'You are Smith Minor, if I remember right.'

'Yes, sir, I am. How clever of you to recognise me.'

'Tell me, Smith, was it you or your brother who was killed in the war?'

A master was taking a Divinity class and asked a young boy called Tomkins, 'Who blew down the Walls of Jericho, Tomkins?'

'I don't know, sir,' Tomkins replied. 'But I promise it wasn't me.'

The master was furious at what he thought was a cheeky reply and went to see the headmaster.

'I'm sorry to trouble you, sir,' he said, 'but I think you should know that when I asked Tomkins who had blown down the Walls of Jericho, he replied that it wasn't him.'

The headmaster thought for a second, then said, 'Well, I know Tomkins quite well, and if he says he didn't do it, then I'm inclined to believe him.' The headmaster then rang up the school bursar and told him that there had been some damage done to the Walls of Jericho.

'Very well, Head. Just send me the details of the damage and I'll get it repaired.'

Some parents were looking over a prospective school for their son. The wife asked the headmaster, 'Is there any drug problem in the school?'

'No,' said the headmaster. 'He'll be able to get as much as he wants here.'

The headmaster of Temple Grove School in Eastbourne had an eye knocked out when playing squash. He was fitted with a glass eye in its place. It was so good that one of the boys asked the matron how she was so sure that it *was* a glass eye.

'Oh,' she said. 'I was talking to him one day and it came out in the conversation.'

Teacher: 'Johnny, name three inventions which have helped man get up in the world.'
Johnny: 'The escalator, the lift and the alarm clock.'

F

for the Forces

During the war, a man who was called up failed to pass the eyesight test. He couldn't even read the top line on the chart. So he was excused service. The doctor who had tested him dropped into a cinema on the way home, and to his surprise saw the man sitting in the row in front of him, obviously enjoying the film. He leant forward and tapped the man on the shoulder. 'Haven't I seen you somewhere before?' he asked.

The man turned round and immediately recognised him. 'Ah, kind sir,' he said. 'Could you possibly tell me if this bus goes to Victoria?'

A young soldier in Germany was getting very homesick for his new bride he had had to leave behind in England. She sent him a telegram which read: 'Not getting any. Better come home at once.' He went to see his Commanding Officer and showed him the telegram. He was given immediate compassionate leave. What he didn't tell the CO was that he had altered the punctuation in the telegram.

Officer on an exercise at Royal Military Academy, Sandhurst: 'Brown, if you were in charge of a platoon defending this ridge, and suddenly you saw ten enemy tanks approaching you up the hill, what steps would you take?'
Brown: 'Bloody long ones, sir.'

A commanding officer was addressing his troops before embarking for an overseas posting. He was stressing the dangers of VD abroad. 'Why spoil your health for just ten minutes' pleasure? Any questions?' A young soldier held up his hand.
CO: 'Yes, what do you want to know?'
Young soldier: 'Please sir? How do you make it last that long?'

A very ugly officer had done wonderful work when attached to the Free French Army. He would have been given the Croix de Guerre, but the French could not find a general prepared to kiss him.

At a regimental dinner a few years after the war, one officer said to another, 'Nice to see you, old boy. How are you?'
'Oh, I'm all right, but feeling rather frustrated with my sex life. I haven't made love to a woman since 1945.'
'Well,' said the first officer, looking at his watch. 'I don't know what you're worried about. It's only 20.15 now.'

A young subaltern joined his new regiment and was warmly welcomed by his commanding officer.
CO: 'Welcome to the regiment. So that you can get to know everybody, I've arranged a party in the mess tonight. A little drink never did anyone any harm.'
Subaltern: 'I'm sorry, sir, but I don't drink.'
CO: 'Don't worry about that then, on Wednesday night we'll get a few girls up to the mess from the NAAFI. A bit of slap and tickle does one a power of good.'
Subaltern: 'Sorry, sir. I don't approve of that sort of thing.'
CO: (looking at the subaltern quizzically) 'Er ... you aren't by any chance a queer, are you?'
Subaltern: 'Certainly not, sir.'
CO: 'Pity. You won't enjoy Saturday night either.'

A desert patrol got lost and were wandering around for days. Their rations soon ran out and their young commander told them that there was no more food left. He said, 'I've got two bits of news for you, one bad, one good. The bad news is that from now on we'll have to eat camel dung. The good news is that there's a lot of it.'

An officer was appointed to be the Military Attaché in Moscow. He had to attend a lot of official functions. At one of them he sat next to a smashing blonde – the only really beautiful girl he had seen since he had arrived in Russia. After a few vodkas the officer began to chat up the blonde who seemed to encourage him with a smile. A little later he got a bit daring and put his hand on her knee. She smiled sweetly at him. Thus encouraged, he ran his hand up the inside of her thigh. This time she didn't smile but quickly wrote something on the menu and handed it to him. It read: 'Careful how you go from now on' – signed, Carruthers, MI5.

G

for Golf and football

A very keen golfer went on a cruise. The ship was wrecked in a storm and the golfer was washed up on to a desert island. He was apparently the only survivor and was alone for about three days. Then a raft came into sight and on it was a glamorous woman with a wonderful figure. She only had enough on to cover her confusion. She stepped ashore and was warmly greeted by the lone golfer and they were soon getting on handsomely together.

The woman cuddled up to him and stroked his bare chest. 'Would you like to play around with me?' she whispered in his ear.

'I would, very much,' replied the golfer. 'But I'm afraid my clubs went down with the ship.'

A young man was due to play golf with his girlfriend. Before the game he went to the professional's shop and bought a couple of golf balls. He put them in his trouser pocket and met his girlfriend on the first tee. She noticed the bulge in his pocket and asked him what it was.

'It's only golf balls,' the young man replied.

'Oh,' she said, 'I'm sorry. Is it something like tennis elbow?'

An optimistic golfer always wore two pairs of socks whenever he played golf – just in case he ever got a hole in one.

A man had just played a game of golf at a strange golf course and rushed off to have a quick shower before going off to an important business appointment. He took his flannel into the shower and, after washing himself, was just about to step out to find a towel when, to his horror, he heard the sound of ladies' voices. He peeped through the shower curtain and saw two elderly ladies and a smashing young blonde. He realised that he had gone into the ladies' shower room by mistake. But he had to get out of the shower as he had this important meeting to go to. So he thought that the only thing to do was to cover his face with the flannel and make a dash for it. He emerged stealthily from the shower and ran quickly past the three ladies, his face hidden by his flannel.

'I wonder who that was?' said one of the elderly ladies.

'Well, it wasn't my husband,' said the other.

'And it certainly wasn't mine,' said the first lady.

'And I can assure you,' said the blonde, 'that it wasn't any member of this club, either.'

A golfer used regularly to slice his drive into a bunker on the right of the green at the short sixteenth. When he died, they found that in his will he had asked that his ashes should be scattered right in the middle of the sixteenth green – something he had never been able to achieve with his ball. So his widow carried the casket up on to the course and stood on the edge of the sixteenth green. She took the lid off the casket and threw her husband's ashes towards the hole in the middle of the green. But it was a windy day and the ashes were blown off to the right, straight into the bunker.

Jimmy Tarbuck tells the story of a friend of his who had a little white poodle. This poodle used to accompany his friend on all his games of golf. If his master did a good drive or sank a long putt, the poodle would stand on his hind legs and applaud with his two front paws.

34

'What happens,' Jimmy asked his friend, 'if you get into a bunker or miss an easy putt?'

'Oh,' said his friend, 'the dog turns somersaults.'

'How many?' asked Jimmy.

'Depends how hard I kick him up the arse,' was the answer.

An unpopular secretary of a golf club was ill in hospital. He received a Get Well card from his committee to which a PS was added: 'The decision to send this card was approved by six votes to five.'

A little boy got lost at a football match. He went up to a policeman and said, 'I've lost my dad.'

'What's he like?' asked the policeman sympathetically.

'Beer and women,' said the boy.

A football team was having a disastrous season and their attendance figures had reached rock bottom. So much so that, before each match started, they used to announce over the PA: 'For the benefit of the players, here are the names of the spectators . . .'

One day a man rang up and asked the manager what time the game started.

'What time can you get here?' was the manager's reply.

A soccer player to a referee: 'What would you do if I said you were a bloody cheat?'

'I'd send you off.'

'Supposing I said I *thought* you were a cheat?'

'Oh, there's nothing I could do about that.'

'Then I *think* you're a bloody cheat.'

Joe Hulme told the story of when Arsenal were playing a 'friendly' against an Italian club in Italy. Playing for Arsenal at half-back was Wilf Copping, a tough player and a formidable tackler. After five minutes' play he tripped up one of the Italians with a ferocious sliding tackle. The referee came up to him and said, 'No more of that, please. This is a friendly game.'

A few minutes later Copping did it again. The referee rushed up and said, 'I warned you just now. Do that again and I will send you off immediately.'

Copping was unable to restrain himself and shortly afterwards did another sliding tackle which got the man instead of the ball. He saw the referee coming towards him with pencil and paper ready. 'Oh bugger off,' said Copping under his breath as the referee approached.

'That is good,' said the referee. 'You apologise, so I do not send you off.'

H

for Hospitals

A lecturer in a teaching hospital was trying to demonstrate the danger of too much drink. To prove his point he placed a live worm in a glass of water and another live worm in a glass of whisky. At the end of his lecture he turned to the two glasses. The worm in the water was wriggling about strongly but the worm in the whisky was still, and obviously stone dead.

The lecturer turned to his audience of medical students and said, 'What is the lesson to be learned from my demonstration?'

A voice from the back quickly replied, 'If you've got worms, drink whisky.'

A man woke up after an operation and through a mist saw a figure standing by his bed.

'Was my operation a success, doctor?' he whispered.

'I don't know, old chap,' said the figure. 'I'm St Peter.'

Charlie Harris, the Nottinghamshire cricketer, once dislocated his shoulder and was sent to hospital. There they tried to put the shoulder back without giving him an anaesthetic. It was so painful that Charlie shouted and screamed.

'Mr Harris,' said one of the nurses, 'do try to be brave. There's a lady having a baby down the corridor and she's not making half the fuss that you are.'

'No,' said Charlie, 'but they're not trying to put it back.'

A man went into hospital for an operation to cure his unfortunate habit of premature ejaculation. His wife rang up the hospital to see whether the operation has been successful. She got on to the surgeon who told her he was afraid that it was still touch and go.

A husband and wife, seventy-one years old, were walking by the hospital and saw a sign: 'Donate to the sperm bank.'

The wife said, 'Go on, Bert, donate!'

'But I'm seventy-one,' said Bert.

'You were all right at Christmas. Go and have a go,' said his wife.

So he went into the hospital, saw the nurse, and said, 'I've come to donate to the sperm bank.' The nurse, rather surprised, asked how old he was, could he do it, was he all right? He answered in the affirmative so she said okay and gave him a small glass jar with a screw top, and said put it in there, and sent him to a cubicle saying she would be back in twenty minutes.

Twenty minutes later she came back and asked how he was getting on.

'I'm having a bit of difficulty,' he said. 'I've tried my right hand, which is my best, I've tried my left hand, I've put it under the hot tap, under the cold tap, and I still can't get the lid off the jar.'

I

for Irish jokes

The pilot of a large jet travelling from New York to London announced over the intercom: 'I'm sorry. We are having engine trouble and I've had to shut down number one engine. Nothing to worry about. It will just mean we shall be fifteen minutes late arriving at Heathrow.'

A few minutes later the pilot came on the intercom again: 'Ladies and gentlemen. I'm sorry. I've just had to shut down number two engine, which is giving a bit of trouble. But don't worry. It will just mean that we shall now be thirty minutes late!'

A few minutes later he came on again. 'It's your captain speaking again. I'm sorry but I've now had to shut down number three engine which means we may be up to an hour late.'

An Irish passenger turned to the man sitting next to him and said, 'I hope he doesn't have to shut down the fourth engine, or we'll be up here all night.'

An Irishman visited his doctor who gave him a bottle of tonic. Two weeks later the Irishman went back to the doctor saying he felt no better.

'Have you been taking the medicine I gave you, Michael?' asked the doctor.

'No,' said Michael.

'Why not?' asked the doctor.

'Well, when I got home I looked at the bottle and there was a label on it which said: "Keep this bottle tightly corked." So I did.'

39

An Irish winner of the famous Tour de France went missing for three weeks. He was found doing a lap of honour.

Two Irishmen were stranded on an iceberg.
  'Look, Paddy,' said one, 'we're saved. Here comes the *Titanic*.'

An Irishman bought a black and white dog as he thought the licence would be cheaper.

An Irish hitchhiker got up early and made an early start on his journey. He wanted to miss the traffic.

An Irishman drove his car into a river because the local policeman told him to dip his headlights.

An Irish motorist got his car stuck in a church door. He'd been told to take his car in for a service.

An Irish cricketer caught a brilliant catch at third slip – but missed it on the action replay.

An Irishman was accused of assaulting a woman and was lined up in an identity parade. The woman was brought into the prison yard where the row of men were standing and the Irishman pointed at her and said, 'That's her.'

An Irishman came home unexpectedly and found his wife in the arms of his best friend. He rushed to the drawer, took out a revolver and pointed it at his head.
  'This is too much,' he cried. 'I'm going to shoot myself.'
  At this, his wife began to laugh.

'I don't know what you're laughing at,' he said to her. 'You're next.'

A notice outside an Irish undertaker's office read: 'Due to the holidays, for the next week we shall be working with a skeleton staff.'

At a level-crossing in Ireland only one of the gates was open. A motorist asked the level-crossing keeper the reason.

'Well, you see, sir, we are half expecting a train.'

Brendan was woken up by the phone ringing. So he got out of bed, went downstairs, and picking up the phone, said, 'Hello?'

'Hello. Is that Connemara double two, double two?'

'No. I'm sorry. This is Connemara two, two, two, two.'

'Oh, I'm sorry to have troubled you.'

'It's all right,' said Brendan. 'I had to come down anyway as the phone was ringing.'

A customer in a Dublin restaurant asked for some coffee at the end of his meal.

'With cream or without?' asked the waiter.

'Without cream, thank you,' said the customer.

After a short delay the waiter returned. 'I'm sorry, sir. There's no more cream. Will you have it without milk?'

An Aer Lingus pilot, when asked for his height and position replied: 'I'm 5ft 4in and sitting in the front seat.'

Why should there be oil in Egypt and potatoes in Ireland? The Irish had first choice.

Two Cork men had always admired alligator shoes so they decided to go alligator shooting. After a few days they had shot quite a few alligators and were very disappointed. One of them said, 'If the next one I shoot hasn't got any shoes, then I'm going home.'

Two Irishmen went into a pub and after ordering two beers took some sandwiches out of their pockets and started to eat them.

'You can't eat your own sandwiches in here,' complained the landlord.

So the two men swapped their sandwiches.

An Irishman rang up London Airport and asked how long the flight to Dublin took.

'Just a minute, sir,' said the operator.

'Thank you,' said the Irishman and rang off.

An Irishman was stopped by a foreign tourist and asked what the yellow line along the side of the street indicated.

'Oh, that means no parking at all.'

'Thank you,' said the tourist. 'But, what do *two* yellow lines mean?'

'Ah,' said the Irishman. 'That means no parking at all, at all.'

J

for Jewish jokes

A Jewish boy and a Catholic boy were having a quarrel.

'Our priest knows more than your rabbi,' said the Catholic.

'He should do,' said the Jew. 'You're always going and telling him everything.'

Abie's wife noticed that he was obviously very worried about something. He couldn't sleep, had lost his appetite and wore a permanent worried look. After a few days she asked him what was wrong.

'It's awful, my dear,' said Abie. 'I owe Benjamin £500. I can't pay it back and I daren't tell him. I don't know what to do.'

'Why don't you ring him up straightaway and tell him so. Then *he'll* do the worrying, not you.'

Isaac told his solicitor, 'Insert a clause in my will which says that when I die I want all my relations to come and dance on my grave. And, by the way, make sure you remember to bury me at sea.'

A landlord knocked on the door of a Jewish tenant.

'Good morning, Samuel,' he said. 'I've come to tell you that I'm going to raise the rent.'

'Thank the good Lord,' said Samuel, 'because I can't.'

A Jewish couple won £250,000 on the pools. They were obviously delighted but the wife had one worry.

'What about all the begging letters?' she asked her husband.

'Continue sending them, my dear,' was his reply.

A man was asked what he thought of an old business friend called Solomon.

'He's a man of rare gifts,' he replied. 'I should know: he's never given me one.'

A lady was weeping by the side of a tombstone in a cemetery. The rabbi came up to try to comfort her.

'It's my husband,' she explained. 'I miss him terribly.'

'Your husband?' queried the rabbi. 'But it says on the gravestone: "To the memory of Rachel Cohen".'

'Yes,' sobbed the lady. 'He always put everything in my name.'

Two Jewish passengers on a cruise received a note in their sumptuous cabin asking them to sit at the captain's table.

'My God,' said the husband to his wife. 'I've paid big money for this cruise and now they ask us to eat with the crew.'

'Mr Goldberg,' said the bank manager on the phone, 'your overdraft now stands at £200. It's been like that since June. What are you going to do about it?'

'What was in it at the end of May?'

'You were in credit with us to the tune of £500.'

'So. Did I ring you?'

K

for Knives and forks

A man got lost in a desert and hadn't had a drink of water for five days. He was in a terrible state: his tongue was hanging out, his clothes were in tatters and he could only muster sufficient strength to drag himself over the sand. Suddenly he saw a caravan, so he crawled up to it and knocked on the door.

The Arab owner opened it and the man croaked out, 'Water, water! Please give me some water.'

'Sorry,' said the Arab. 'We have no water. Only ties. MCC tie, the Geoff Boycott testimonial tie, Cornhill tie – any tie you like.'

'No, no,' said the man as he crawled away. 'All I want is water.'

He struggled on a few more hundred yards and came on another caravan. Once again an Arab came to the door.

'Water, water,' croaked the man even more huskily. 'I must have water.'

'Sorry,' said the Arab. 'We have no water. Only ties. The Primary Club tie, Lord's Taverners' tie, the Free Forrester tie. Any tie you like.'

'No, no. I only want water,' blurted out the man, his tongue even more swollen in the heat.

He crawled away and had the same experience at two other caravans. It was ties, ties, ties – no water. In despair he crawled to the top of a sand dune and, looking over the top, saw a verdant golf course laid out before him with lush fairways and green. Surely, he thought, there must be water here. So, with one last effort he dragged himself up to the door of the club house and knocked.

A steward appeared and asked him what he wanted.

'I want water, water. Let me in, let me in,' he pleaded.

'I'm sorry, sir,' said the steward. 'You can't come in here without a tie.'

Diner: 'Waiter, there's a fly in my soup!'
Waiter: 'It's all right, sir, he won't live long in that stuff.'

Waiter: 'Would you like aperitif, sir?'
Diner: 'No thanks. I always use my own dentures.'

Waiter: 'Waiter, have you got frogs' legs?'
Diner: 'Yes, sir.'
Waiter: 'Well, hop over there and get me the mustard, please.'

Waiter: 'Would you like a salad, sir?'
Diner: 'Yes please. I'll have a honeymoon salad.'
Waiter: 'Honeymoon salad, sir? What is that?'
Diner: 'Lettuce alone without dressing.'

'Waiter, do you serve crabs in this restaurant?'

'Yes, sir, sit down. We serve anyone here.'

A waiter was scratching his bottom.

'Excuse me asking,' exclaimed a concerned lady diner, 'but have you got haemorrhoids?'

'No, madam, I'm sorry,' replied the waiter. 'Only what's on the menu.'

'Waiter, what on earth is this soup?'

'It's bean soup, sir.'

'I don't care what it's *been*, what is it now?'

A waiter brought a customer the lobster which he had ordered. But it only had one claw. The customer noticed this and asked where the other claw was. The waiter had to think quickly.

'When they arrived this morning they were still alive, and two of them started fighting, and this one lost a claw in the fight.'

'Okay,' said the customer. 'Then bring me the winner.'

The waiter presented the menu to a young man and his girlfriend.

'What do you suggest?' asked the young man. 'I've only got £10.'

'Another restaurant, sir,' said the waiter.

A guest sitting at the top table at a club dinner got hardly any wine to drink all evening. But he got his own back. When he stood up to propose the health of Absent Friends he coupled this with the name of the wine waiter.

'Waiter, how long will my sausages be?'

'I don't know, sir. We never measure them.'

Diner: 'Waiter! This coffee tastes like earth.'

Waiter: 'I'm not surprised, sir. It was only ground this morning.'

Waiter: 'How did you find the steak, sir?'

Diner: 'I just lifted up a few peas and there it was.'

The proprietor of a restaurant was surprised to read in a newspaper that its food critic had awarded the chef a Black Belt for cooking. He wrote and asked the critic to explain this unusual honour. Back came the reply: 'In your restaurant, it's one chop and you're dead.'

L

for the Law

A judge was about to sentence a prisoner who had been found guilty.

'Is there anything you want to say before I sentence you, my man?' he asked.

'Bugger all, m'lud,' replied the prisoner.

The judge, who was a bit hard of hearing, called down to his clerk of the court, 'What did he say?'

'Bugger all, m'lud,' answered the clerk.

'No,' said the judge, 'he definitely said something. I saw him move his lips.'

Three magistrates were trying a case of indecent assault. It was a hot afternoon and the courtroom was stuffy. On the Chairwoman's right was an alert businessman and on her left was a retired colonel with a bristling white moustache. He began to nod off and was soon fast asleep as the Chairwoman asked the young woman in the witness box to write down what the accused man had said to her. The girl wrote something down on a piece of paper which was handed up to the Chairwoman, who read it and then gently nudged the sleeping colonel to wake him up. He gave a slight snort and woke up to find the following note being passed to him by the Chairwoman: 'I'm feeling randy. What about coming back to my place for a quick one?'

He read it with horror and handed it back to the Chairwoman, whispering, 'Madam, control yourself. You must be out of your mind!'

What was the nickname given to a well-known judge who had lost a thumb? Mr Justice Fingers.

'Remember you are on oath,' said the judge to the third party in a divorce case. 'Answer me this. Have you ever slept with this woman?'
    'Not a wink, m'lud,' was the reply.

A man suffering from amnesia was found wandering in the streets by the police. When questioned he said he didn't know where he came from. So they took him to the police station, and, to keep him occupied, gave him a copy of the *Sun* to read. He immediately turned to page three and became very excited. The sergeant behind the desk said, 'He is obviously a Bristol man.'

A householder rang up his local police to report that a large hole had appeared in the road opposite his house. The police are now looking into it.

'Can you see me across the street, officer?'
    'I'm afraid I can't, madam. I've left my glasses at home.'

A man was visiting a prison when one of the warders came up to him and asked him if he would buy a ticket for the Governor's ball.
    'I'm sorry,' said the man. 'I'm afraid I don't dance.'
    'It's not a dance, it's a raffle,' explained the warder.

There had been a lot of escapes from a certain prison in recent weeks. So the chef in the prison canteen asked the Governor, 'How many will there be for lunch today, sir?'

Judge: 'Is this the first time you've been up before me?'
Prisoner: 'I don't know, m'lud. What time do you usually get up?'

A farmer was talking to his solicitor before a case. The solicitor assured the farmer that he would get him off.

'But wouldn't it help if I sent the judge a couple of ducks?' asked the farmer.

'Good gracious, no. That would go against you. The judge would consider it bribery.'

After the case the solicitor congratulated the farmer when he was found not guilty. 'There you are,' he said. 'I told you I would get you off.'

'Yes, I know,' said the farmer. 'I sent the two ducks in the other chap's name.'

M

for Miscellaneous

When his wife died a Yorkshireman asked the stonemason to carve on her tombstone the words: 'She was Thine.'

Some weeks later, after the funeral, he went up to the churchyard and, to his annoyance, saw the following words on his wife's tombstone: 'She was Thin.'

He rang up the stonemason and complained that an 'e' had been left out. The mason apologised and said that he would rectify the mistake as soon as possible.

A week later the husband returned to his wife's grave and read the alteration that had been made: 'E, she was Thin.'

A man jumped off a skyscraper and miraculously fell to the pavement unhurt. As he got up and brushed himself down, a passerby rushed up to him and asked, 'What happened?'

'I don't know,' was the reply. 'I've only just arrived.'

Early one morning a young man took a young woman for a walk in the fields. The sun was up and the grass was damp. He knelt down to test it.

'Some dew,' he said.

'Some don't,' she said, 'Good morning.'

A rather short-sighted social worker knocked on the door of a house. A small boy came to the door. The conversation went as follows: 'Is your father in?'

'No, he went out when my mother came in.'

'Is your mother in, then?'

'No, she went out when my brother came in.'

'Can I see him then, please?'

'No. I'm afraid not. He went out when I came in.'

'So, you are left in charge of the house?'

'Oh, no. This isn't our house. It's our outside lavatory.'

The rich lady returned home from a ball. She rang the bell for her footman and when he appeared she said, 'Edward, take off my shoes,' and he did. Then she said: 'Edward, take off my coat,' and he did. 'Take off my dress,' and he did. 'And now take off my underclothes,' and he did. 'And now, Edward,' she said, 'if you wish to remain in my service, you are never to wear any of my clothes again.'

A man went into a pub.

'Good evening, sir,' said the landlord. 'What would you like to drink?'

'A large whisky, thank you.'

The landlord said: 'That will be 90p please.'

'Oh, no,' said the man. 'I distinctly remember you inviting me to have a drink. I thought it was very kind of you.'

The landlord turned to another customer, who was a solicitor, and asked for support. The solicitor said that he was sorry, but the landlord had definitely made an offer and the man had accepted it, so he did not have to pay. The landlord was furious and turned the man out of the pub, telling him never to come back again. But about ten minutes later the man reappeared.

'I thought I told you never to come back,' said the landlord.

'I've never been here before in my life,' said the man.

'Then you must have a double,' said the landlord.

'Thank you very much, I will, and I'm sure our solicitor friend would like one too.'

The hotel guest wanted a clean towel, so rang the bell which said 'maid'. He rang and rang and after a long delay an elderly porter knocked on his door.

'I've been ringing for ages. Where's the chambermaid?' the guest asked angrily.

'I'm not sure, sir. But I think it comes from the Potteries.'

The local squire and his wife were entertaining their tenants and servants to a Christmas party. The conjuror whom they had engaged approached an elderly gamekeeper.

'Would you be surprised if I brought a live rabbit out of your inside pocket?' he asked the gamekeeper.

'That I would be,' growled the gamekeeper. 'I've got a ruddy ferret in there.'

An English farmer was showing an Australian sheep farmer round his farm. They travelled in his Land Rover and the journey round the five hundred acres or so took almost half an hour. When they got back to the farmhouse the Englishman asked the Australian what he thought about the farm.

'Well, back in Australia, I can get in my car and it will take me four days to go round *my* estate.'

'Yes, I sympathise,' said the Englishman. 'I once had a car like that.'

Robin Hood, in spite of all his daring deeds, was not himself a great archer. When he lay dying he implored his Merry Men to hand him his bow and arrow. He staggered out of bed and aimed at the open window.

'Please bury me wherever the arrow lands.'

So saying he took aim and shot the arrow. They buried him on top of the wardrobe.

Some visitors were going round the Chamber of Horrors at

Madame Tussaud's. An attendant approached one of them and pointed to a woman who was standing still staring at one of the gruesome exhibits.

'Excuse me, sir, is that lady anything to do with you?'

'Yes,' said the man. 'She's my mother-in-law.'

'Well, please keep her moving. We're stocktaking,' said the attendant.

A man rang up a friend and heard a lot of voices in the background when the friend answered the telephone.

'I'm sorry to bother you. Are you entertaining?'

'No, actually I'm rather boring.'

A smartly dressed man in a bowler hat was walking through St James's Park, when he was suddenly caught short. He had to rush behind a tree to do the necessary. When he had finished he heard one of the park-keepers approaching, so hurriedly covered up what he had done with his bowler hat.

'What's going on here, sir?' asked the keeper.

'Oh,' said the man. 'I've just found a very rare bird and have managed to trap it under my bowler hat. It's so rare, I must go straight off to the zoo to check what it is, and where it comes from. Could you very kindly stand by it while I'm away, and see that no one interferes with it?'

The keeper agreed and stood on guard by the bowler hat as the man dashed off to get a taxi to the zoo.

A crowd soon collected at this strange sight of a bowler hat being guarded by the keeper. They all asked him what it was all about, and he explained that under the hat was a very rare bird.

'Can we have a look at it?' they asked him.

'No, certainly not. It might escape and I promised to guard it.'

The crowd weren't satisfied and went on badgering him. 'Why not have a quick peep yourself and see what it looks like?'

After a lot of persuasion, the keeper agreed and got down

on his knees, and lifted the rim of the bowler a few inches and quickly put it down again.

'What's it look like, what's its colour and what sort of bird is it?' they asked him.

The keeper got to his feet and told them, 'I don't know about the bird, but someone hasn't half frightened it.'

A man unfortunately broke wind when speaking to his hostess at a dinner party.

'How dare you break wind in front of my wife,' said the host.

'Sorry,' said the guest. 'I didn't know that it was her turn!'

A man tried to gatecrash a fancy dress dance. He was dressed as a pair of jump leads. After a bit of an argument the steward on the door said: 'All right you can go in, so long as you don't start anything.'

A tramp knocked on the door of a large house. A grand old lady opened the door.

'What do you want, my man?' she asked.

'Please, ma'm, I'm very hungry. I haven't eaten for four days. Can I have something to eat?'

'Certainly,' she said. 'Do you like *cold* rice pudding?'

'Yes, yes, ma'm, I do. It's my favourite.'

'Well, come back tomorrow. It's still hot!'

A man called his house Lautrec, because it only had two loos.

Little boy: 'Mummy, does God use our bathroom?
Mummy: 'No, of course he doesn't, dear.'
Little boy: 'Then why in the mornings does Daddy bang on the door and shout: 'God, are you still in there?'

A man bought a pair of shoes two sizes too small for him. When asked why, he explained, 'My wife has left me, my business has gone bust, and my twelve-year-old daughter is pregnant. The only pleasure I now get out of life is when I take off my shoes at the end of the day.'

Billy Bennett: 'Never despise a bow-legged girl. She may be on pleasure bent.'

'I went out with twins last night.'
  'Any luck?'
  'Yes and no.'

Extracts from genuine letters sent to the Ministry of Pensions:
'I am glad to say that my husband that was missing is now dead.'
'In reply to your letter, I have already co-habited with your officer, so far nothing has happened.'
'Sir, I am forwarding my marriage certificate and two children, one of which is a mistake as you will see. Unless I get husband's money I will be forced to live an immortal life.'
'In answer to your letter I have given birth to a boy weighing 10 lbs, is this satisfactory?'
'You have changed my boy to a girl, will this make any difference?'
'Please send some money as I have fallen into errors with my landlord.'
'In accordance with your instructions I have given birth to twins in the enclosed envelope.'
'I want money as quick as you can send it. I have been in bed with the doctor for a week and he doesn't seem to be doing any good. If things don't improve I shall have to send for another doctor.'
'Milk is needed for the baby and father is unable to supply it.'

Girl to boyfriend as he came out of the sea: 'Did the water come up to your expectations?'

'No, darling, it didn't. I was only paddling.'

A flasher told his friends that he was going to retire. He then changed his mind and said he had decided to stick it out for another year.

A Pole went to have his eyes tested. The oculist showed him the chart with the lines of letters, large at the top, but getting smaller and smaller until the bottom line was very difficult to decipher.

'Can you read the bottom line?' the oculist asked the Pole.

The Pole had a quick look. 'Read it?' he said. 'He's my best friend.'

N

for 'Ntertainment

Jimmy James was one of my favourite comedians. He kept a deadpan face, puffed continuously at cigarettes, and had a stuttering walk, 'giving' occasionally at the knees. One of his stooges was called Eli, and Jimmy used to tell him that he had plans for him to become an intrepid parachutist. Eli would be flown twenty thousand feet into the air and would then drop through the roof of the theatre.

'Don't pull the rip-cord until you are ten feet above the stalls,' said Jimmy.

'But what will happen if the parachute doesn't open?' asked Eli.

'You can jump ten feet, can't you?' was Jimmy's reply.

Tommy Cooper: 'Last night I dreamt I ate a ten-pound marsh-mallow. When I woke up the pillow was gone.'

Tommy Cooper *after igniting an explosive in a cake-tin:* 'Just a flash in the pan.'

Tommy Trinder: A man had lost his way during the blackout in the war. He asked a passerby in Whitehall, 'Please can you tell me which side the War Office is on?'

'Ours, I hope,' was the reply.

The popular pianist at a pub had retired and the landlord put up

58

a notice advertising the job. One day a dirty-looking tramp came in. His clothes were in tatters and there was an enormous hole in the seat of his trousers. He saw the piano in the corner and immediately went over, sat down on the wicker stool and started to play. He played beautifully, modern tunes, old tunes, classics – the lot. The customers began to gather round, applauding him and asking for their special favourites to be played. He seemed to know all the requests, but if he wasn't sure he just asked the customer to sing the opening bars and he soon picked it up. The landlord was delighted, took him a pint of beer, and in spite of his terrible clothes and the hole in his trousers, decided to give him the job. The requests continued to flow in until a little old lady, who had been sitting quietly sipping a port and lemon, approached the tramp and tapped him on the shoulder.

'I say,' she whispered confidentially, 'do you know your balls are hanging through the wicker stool?'

'No, I don't, madam,' said the tramp. 'But if you hum it, I'll soon be able to pick it up.'

A short-sighted, bespectacled man was having a drink in the theatre bar before going into the auditorium. To his surprise there was a notice at the exit of the bar which said: 'Glasses are not allowed in the auditorium.' So he took off his specs and had a miserable evening.

A comedian found that he was playing to smaller and smaller houses. It got so bad that at the first house at one music hall there was no audience at all. A 'kind' friend suggested that he should write to the Pope and ask *him* for an audience.

Woman in cinema box office: 'That's the fifth ticket you've bought.'
Customer: 'I know. But the chap on the entrance to the cinema keeps tearing them in half.'

A man rang up the wife of his friend, Jack, who was a famous after-dinner speaker.

'How's Jack?' he asked her.

'I don't know,' was the reply. 'I haven't spoken to him for three days.'

'Has he been away, then?'

'No. I didn't like to interrupt.'

A speaker had just finished what he thought was one of his best after-dinner speeches. When he had finished a drunk went over to him and said, 'That's the most boring speech I have ever heard in my life.'

The chairman, who hadn't heard what he said, dragged him away and said to the speaker, 'Sorry about old Tomkins. But pay no attention to what he says. When he's drunk he only repeats what everyone else is saying.'

Another speaker, famous for his long speeches, went on and on. His audience could stand no more, and gradually began to drift quietly away. The speaker finally looked up and saw there was only one man left in the hall. Regardless, the speaker was determined to finish his prepared speech. When at last he came to the end he went up to the lone man and thanked him for being polite enough to stay to the end.

'Oh no,' said the man. 'I'm only the caretaker, and I have to wait to lock up.'

A speaker at a dinner went on and on. After about forty minutes a drunk diner picked up a bottle and threw it at him. Unfortunately, it missed the speaker and hit the chairman on the head. The chairman was momentarily knocked out, but as soon as he came round he said, 'Hit me again – I can still hear him.'

O

for Office life

A businessman was boasting to a friend how successful he was. 'When I became chairman of my present firm a year ago it was on the edge of a precipice. Now it's taken a giant step forward.'

Secretary: 'The invisible man is outside.'
Boss: 'Well tell him I can't see him today.'

A man in an office was always boasting that he was an expert at everything in their business. One of his colleagues got fed up with this and asked him if he really knew what 'expert' meant – 'Ex' meant you've had it, and 'spurt' is a drip under pressure.

A businessman was a very keen cricketer. On his desk he had three trays marked IN, OUT and LBW. When asked why LBW he explained, 'Let the Buggers Wait.'

A businessman from Bombay was changing some rupees in a London bank, and complained about the rate of exchange which he had been given. 'Why is the rate so bad?'
  'Oh, just fluctuations,' replied the clerk.
  'Well, fluctu-Europeans too,' said the Indian.

A notice pinned up on an office noticeboard:

WORKPLACE RULES

DUE TO EXCESSIVE ABSENTEEISM THE FOLLOW-
ING MUST BE NOTED:–

1 SICKNESS – A Doctor's Certificate is no longer valid, if you can get to the doctor you can work.

2 DEATH (your own) – This is an acceptable reason for absence; however, two weeks' notice must be given, otherwise all pension rights will be forfeited.

3 DEATH (someone else's) – This is no excuse as there is nothing further you can do for them. No time off will be allowed for funerals, etc.

4 OPERATIONS – No leave will be allowed for visits to hospital. We employed you as you are: if bits are removed this will be a breach of your contract with us.

5 VISITS TO THE LOO – Too much time is being wasted; in future a strict rota will be maintained. You are allowed two visits a day at a time determined by your name, i.e., 'A' 10.00–10.05, 'B' 10.05–10.10, etc.

6 MEAL/DRINK BREAKS – These have been discontinued. You are all overweight and becoming too slow to work.

7 HEATING – It has been observed that you move quicker when cold trying to keep warm. No heating will be turned on in future.

COMPANY MOTTO – HAVE A NICE DAY

Caller on the telephone: 'Can I speak to Mr Smith, please?'
Secretary: 'No. I'm very sorry. He is not here this afternoon.'
Caller: 'Doesn't he work in the afternoons then?'
Secretary: 'Oh no. It's in the morning he doesn't work. He doesn't *come in* in the afternoon.'

62

Manager to office boy: 'Thompson, you're late. You should have been here at nine-thirty.'
Thompson: 'Why sir? What happened?'

'That's a very expensive coat for a struggling typist.'
'Yes. I decided to give up struggling.'

A man rushed into an office. 'Do you believe in free speech?' he shouted to the man behind the desk.

'Yes, of course I do,' said the office worker, slightly alarmed.

'Right, let me use your telephone.'

Memo from Managing Director to Works Director:
Tomorrow morning there will be a total eclipse of the sun at nine o'clock. This is something which we cannot see happen every day, so let the workforce line up outside in their best clothes to watch it. To mark the occasion of this rare occurrence I will personally explain it to them. If it is raining we shall not be able to see it very well and in that case the workforce should assemble in the canteen.

Memo from Works Director to General Works Manager:
By order of the Managing Director there will be a total eclipse of the sun at nine o'clock tomorrow morning. If it is raining we shall not be able to see it very well on site, in our best clothes. In that case the disappearance of the sun will be followed through in the canteen. This is something that we cannot see happen every day.

Memo from General Works Manager to Works Manager:
By order of the Managing Director we shall follow through, in our best clothes, the disappearance of the sun in the canteen at nine o'clock tomorrow morning. The Managing Director will tell us whether it is going to rain. This is something which we cannot see happen every day.

Memo from Works Manager to Foreman:
If it is raining in the canteen tomorrow morning, which is something that we cannot see happen every day, our Managing Director, in his best clothes, will disappear at nine o'clock.

Message from Foreman to Shop Floor:
Tomorrow morning at nine o'clock our Managing Director will disappear. It's a pity that we cannot see this happen every day.

Three bank clerks were always playing cards during business hours when the manager wasn't looking. One day he saw them playing, so he thought he would teach them a lesson and give them a fright. He rang the alarm bell three times, but despite this they went on playing. After a couple of minutes the barman from the pub opposite brought over three pints of beer.

'What's your brother doing these days?'
 'Nothing.'
 'Oh, I thought he had applied for that job at Methuen's.'
 'Yes, he got the job.'
 'He's lucky. *My* brother's unemployed and living above his income.'
 'How does he manage that?'
 'He's got a flat over the Social Security office.'

A man who worked in an office was always interfering in other people's business. He would make suggestions, offer advice and generally try to organise everything that went on. He even went so far as to try out his ideas on the managing director, who somewhat naturally resented it, and gave the man an almighty rocket. But the man misunderstood what he meant and rushed home to his wife.

'Darling, I've got some great news. I've been promoted. The managing director has made me his sexual adviser.'

'Oh, wonderful darling. I'm *so* pleased. What did he say to you to break the news?'

'Well he rose to his feet and accompanied me to the door, talking so fast that I couldn't hear much of what he was saying. But I did hear the important part. As I went out of the door he said, "When I want your f*****g advice, I'll ask for it." '

P

for Politics

Two MPs were talking in the tea room of the House of Commons.

'I'm not sure what to do about the Abortion Bill. What do you think I should do?'

'Oh, pay it at once, before someone finds out,' his companion replied.

Q
for Questions

The quizmaster asked, 'What were the first words that Eve said to Adam when she saw him in the Garden of Eden?'

The young lady contestant thought for a moment, and shook her head. 'That's a hard one,' she said to the quizmaster.

He replied: 'Correct. Two marks.'

Q: When should you never yell for help?
A: When you are hanging on by your teeth.

Q: What is one word to describe a very small mother?
A: Minimum.

Q: What's the definition of an archaeologist?
A: A man whose career is in ruins.

Q: How do porcupines make love?
A: Very carefully.

Q: What did the Leaning Tower of Pisa say to Big Ben?
A: If you've got the time, I've got the inclination.

Q: Why did the squirrel swim on his back?
A: To keep his nuts dry.

A questionnaire was sent out to a lot of men, asking them how they liked ladies' legs. Ten per cent replied that they liked them fat. Ten per cent said that they liked them thin. Eighty per cent said that they liked something in between.

Q: Where does Thursday come before Wednesday?
A: In the dictionary.

Q: Why didn't the skeleton go to the ball?
A: Because he had nobody to go with.

R

for Religion

A bishop was offered some wine at a dinner.

'No, thank you,' he said. 'I'd rather commit adultery than drink.'

A man sitting next to him, who had already taken some wine, murmured to his companion, 'I wish I had known. I didn't realise there was an alternative.'

Two bishops were in London to attend a week's synod at Church House. They were having tea and crumpets in front of the fire at the Athenaeum, discussing how they were going to deal with the subject of the next day's conference. It was an awkward topic for a bishop – pre-marital sex.

'For instance,' said one bishop, 'I never slept with my wife before I married her. Did you?'

'I can't remember,' said the other bishop. 'What was her maiden name?'

A bishop had a bad reputation in his diocese for preaching long and very boring sermons. His reputation spread rapidly, because each Sunday he used to visit a different parish to preach. One day he arrived at five to eleven at a small country church and was welcomed by the vicar who was looking a bit flustered. He led the bishop into the church and, to the bishop's surprise and annoyance, there were only three people in the congregation.

'Didn't you warn them that I was coming?' he asked the

vicar angrily.

'I certainly did not, bishop,' replied the vicar. 'But I shall do my very best to find out who did!'

A vicar was very fond of his drink. A lady parishioner sent him a bottle of cherry brandy for Christmas. When giving out the notices at matins he concluded, 'I'd also like to thank Mrs Smith for her gift of fruit and the spirit in which it was given.'

A bishop was presenting the prizes at a school. He got tired of saying the same words of congratulations to each recipient. So, when a pretty blonde girl came up to receive her prize he thought he would try something different.

'What are you going to do when you leave school, my dear?' he asked.

'Well, bishop,' she replied, blushing. 'I was going home for tea with my mother. But I could cancel that.'

A vicar thought that a spot of advertising for his church would not do any harm. So, he put up a big poster with the slogan: 'If you are tired of sin, please step inside.'

The next day, he saw scribbled underneath it: 'But if not, telephone St John's Wood 29591.'

A young man about to be married asked his vicar whether he had any strong objections to sex before marriage.

After a moment's hesitation, the vicar replied, 'No, not really. So long as it doesn't keep the wedding guests waiting.'

In pre-war days a vicar was driving his bishop round the parish in a pony cart. As they were bowling along the village street the pony let out a rude noise.

'Sorry about that, bishop,' said the vicar, slightly embarrassed.

'Not to worry,' said the bishop. 'If you hadn't mentioned it I'd have thought it was the pony.'

One of our archbishops sailed on the *Queen Elizabeth* on his first visit to America. On arrival at New York he was surrounded by reporters. The first question was from a tough Brooklyn reporter who asked the archbishop if he intended to visit any of New York's infamous strip clubs.

The archbishop thought carefully before answering. '*Are* there any strip clubs in New York?'

The next day's headlines in the press read: ARCHBISHOP'S FIRST QUESTION: 'ARE THERE ANY STRIP CLUBS IN NEW YORK?'

A man used to go to the same barber regularly once a fortnight. He was an excellent barber, but had the annoying habit of belittling anything his customer said. One fortnight the customer said he had bought a new car.

'What sort?' asked the barber.

'A Ford,' said the customer.

'Oh,' said the barber. 'Never get a Ford. Get any other car, but *not* a Ford.'

The following fortnight the customer was saying that he had just bought a new fridge and mentioned the name.

Immediately the barber said, 'You've bought one of those? They always break down. Any other make but *not* that.'

The following fortnight the customer said he was going on holiday to Rome.

'Why choose Rome?' asked the barber.

'Well,' said the customer. 'It's my ambition to see the Pope and, if possible, to be spoken to by him.'

'You're crazy to go to Rome. Anywhere else, but *not* Rome. And, anyway, I bet you £50 that the Pope doesn't talk to you.'

The customer was so fed up that he rashly accepted the challenge. A month later he went to the barber, who promptly asked him how he had got on in Rome and reminded him of the £50 bet.

'Oh no,' said the customer. 'You owe *me* £50. The Pope *did* speak to me.'

The barber was incredulous. 'How and where did it happen?' he asked.

'Well,' said the customer, 'I was wandering around St Peter's Square one day hoping to catch sight of the Pope when, to my surprise and delight, I saw him walking towards me. I was even more surprised when he stopped and addressed a few words to me.'

'Go on. What did he say?' asked the barber in disbelief.

'Oh, he just said quietly to me: "Do tell me. Where on earth did you get that terrible haircut?" '

A clergyman prided himself on his spontaneity and told a friend that he could preach a sermon on any subject at a moment's notice. His friend challenged him to do so the following Sunday and said he would put a piece of paper with the required subject in the pulpit, just before the service.

When the time for the sermon came the clergyman mounted the pulpit and there found the promised slip of paper. On it was written just one word: 'Constipation'. The clergyman paused for a moment and then said, 'My text is taken from the Book of Exodus, Chapter 34. "And Moses took the tablets and went up into the mountain." '

A rich English Roman Catholic had one wish. He wanted to meet the Pope personally and was prepared to spend as long as necessary in Rome until he did so. So every day he joined the crowds in St Peter's Square and occasionally saw the Pope on his balcony. But that was the nearest he ever got. He was beginning to despair when one day he went to the British Embassy to sign the ambassador's book. A young attaché saw him sign it and asked if he would like a ticket for a garden party which the Pope was giving in the Vatican the next day. The only snag was that he would have to wear full morning dress. The man was delighted and said the clothes were no problem. So he was given a ticket, went off to the equivalent of Moss Bros and hired himself some morning clothes.

The next day he went to the Vatican dressed in his morning suit and top hat. He stood in a line of guests waiting for the Pope to appear. The guests were drawn up in two lines facing each other, so that the Pope could walk down one line and then turn and go back along the other line. Finally he appeared, to great applause. The Englishman was standing there hopefully as the Pope proceeded down the line. But he spoke to nobody, just waved his hands in a sort of blessing and proceeded to the end of the line.

There, to the surprise of the Englishman, stood a dirty-looking tramp in the most dreadful old clothes – a real contrast to the immaculately dressed throng. The Englishman was even more surprised when he saw the Pope put his hands on the tramp's shoulders and whisper something in his ear. The Englishman thought quickly to himself: obviously the Pope will only talk to someone who is poor, down and out and needing special words of comfort.

So he quickly rushed up the line, got hold of the tramp and asked him if he would change clothes with him for a thousand lire. The tramp couldn't believe his ears and instantly agreed. So they went behind a large bush and quickly exchanged clothes. Dressed now as the tramp, the Englishman just had time to rush to the end of the second line, down which the Pope was proceeding. His heart beat faster as the Pope came nearer and then, to his utter joy, the Pope approached him and put both hands on his shoulders – just as he had done to the tramp. The Englishman couldn't believe it. The Pope was going to talk to him. His wish had come true. And here it was, the Pope was whispering in his ear . . .

'I thought I told you just now to bugger off!'

Moses spent several days and nights in the mountain 'nego-
tiating' with God about the Commandments. One morning he
came rushing down the mountain and summoned the multitude.

'Gather round,' he cried. 'I've got two bits of news about the
Commandments. One good, one bad. The good news is that we
have got them down to ten.'

There were loud cheers from the multitude.

'What about the bad news then, Moses?' they shouted.

'Well,' he said, 'the bad news is that adultery is still in!'

A vicar lost his bicycle and suspected that someone must have
stolen it. So he told the verger that on the next Sunday when
he was reading out the Ten Commandments he would pause
significantly after number eight, 'Thou shalt not steal.' He asked
the verger to watch the congregation carefully and see whether
he could spot anyone looking guilty.

After the service the verger said to the vicar, 'You never
paused as you said you would after the eighth Commandment.'

'No,' said the vicar. 'I didn't. Because when I read out the
seventh Commandment I remembered where I had left my bicycle.'

In a match between two teams of clergy the local bishop opened
the innings. A young curate was the opening bowler, and in due
deference to the bishop's office sent up a slow half-volley with the
intention of helping the portly bishop to 'get off the mark'. The
bishop smote the ball right out of the ground and turned to the
young curate, saying, 'I'm sorry, young man, but I seem to have
hit you out of your parish.'

The curate grinned sheepishly, and feeling rather peeved,
walked slowly back to his mark. He turned, ran in, and sent
down a vicious bumper. This hit the bishop in the midriff and
he collapsed to the ground in agony.

The young curate rushed up and said, 'I'm sorry, m'lord, but I seem to have hit you in the middle of your diocese.'

A man went up to heaven and reported to St Peter at the pearly gates.

'Name, please,' said St Peter.

'Geoffrey Boycott,' was the reply.

St Peter ran his finger down his list of names. 'I'm sorry, Mr Boycott, we've got no reservation for you here. You will have to go elsewhere.'

Geoffrey Boycott went off muttering under his breath and came back after a few minutes.

'Excuse me. I don't think you could have heard me all right just now. I am Geoffrey Boycott, late of Yorkshire and England.'

'I'm sorry, sir. We still haven't got a place for you.'

As Boycott walked off, a very old man with a long grey beard walked up to the gates.

'Yes, sir?' said St Peter.

'I am Geoffrey Boycott,' said the old man. 'Can I come in?'

'Certainly, sir,' said St Peter. 'Welcome. We're very glad to see you.'

A man who had been waiting his turn asked St Peter why he had turned away the real Geoffrey Boycott and then immediately welcomed the old man who was obviously only pretending.

'Well, you see, the old man is God and we have to humour Him. He keeps on thinking He's Geoffrey Boycott,' replied St Peter.

A bishop was visiting a primary school.

'I'll give 5p to the boy or girl who tells me who I am,' he proclaimed.

A small boy said, 'Please, sir, you are God.'

'No, I am not,' said the bishop. 'But here's 10p.'

S

for Shopping

A man went into a grocer's shop.
  'I'd like some sauce.'
  'HP?' asked the shopkeeper.
  'No, thanks. I'll pay cash.'

A customer complained to her butcher about the sausages which she had bought from him last week.
  'They were all meat at one end, all bread at the other.'
  'I'm sorry, madam,' said the butcher. 'In these hard times it's difficult to make both ends meat.'

Lady: 'I have come to return this carpet which I bought from you last week. You assured me that it was in mint condition.'
Shopkeeper: 'So it is, madam. Look at that hole in the middle.'

Customer to pretty shop assistant: 'What'll you take off for cash?'
Shop assistant: 'Everything except my earrings.'

A man went into a newsagent's and asked the girl behind the counter, 'Do you keep stationery?'
  'No,' she said, 'I wriggle about a bit.'

A father and his eighteen-year-old son went into a chemist's shop to buy various things. The son asked for a packet of six condoms.

'That's rather excessive, isn't it?' asked the father. 'Why do you want as many as six?'

'Quite easy, Dad. Monday, Tuesday, Wednesday, Thursday, Friday, Saturday.'

'Well, in that case, can I please have twelve?' the father asked the chemist.

'Steady, Dad. Aren't *you* overdoing it now. Why do you need *twelve*?'

'January, February, March, April . . .' replied his father.

Woman in butcher's shop: 'I want four pork chops, please, and make them lean.'
Butcher: 'Certainly, madam. Which way?'

A blind man went into a supermarket with his guide dog. He was obviously very strong because he got hold of the lead and swung the dog round and round his head. The manager of the store came up and asked him what he was doing it for.

'Just having a look around,' he replied.

A man went into a chemist and asked for some rat poison.

'I'm sorry, we don't stock it,' said the assistant. 'Why not try Boots?'

'I want to poison them, not kick them to death,' replied the man.

Q: Why don't they sell Lucozade in Boots?
A: Because it runs through the lace holes.

'Can I have a tablet of soap, please?'
'Certainly, madam. Would you like it scented?'
'No thank you. I'll take it with me.'

Signs seen in shops or elsewhere:
Maternity shop: *You should have danced all night.*
Wine shop: *Thirst come – Thirst served.*
Travel agent's: *Why don't you go away?*
Undertaker's: *Drive carefully – we can wait.*
Church: *Do you know what Hell is? Come and hear our organist on Thursday evening.*
Supermarket: *Choose any cereal – pick out the noise you like.*
Firework factory: *Man wanted to help at firework parties. Must be prepared to go off at short notice.*
Watch repair shop: *Out to unwind. Back in ten minutes.*
Florist, advertising a rose named after a famous sex symbol: *Does well in a bed, but best against a wall.*

A lady had a pet dog which was one of those tiny chihuahuas. Its hair began to fall out so she went to her local chemist and asked him if he had anything to stop hair falling out.

'Certainly, madam,' he said, as he took down a pot of ointment from a shelf. 'Rub this in for two days, but after that there must be no friction. So don't wear a hat for a fortnight.'

'Oh,' said the lady, 'it's not for my hair, it's for my chihuahua.'

'In that case,' said the chemist. 'Don't ride a bike for a week.'

A man went into a fish shop.

'Plaice, please,' he said.

'I'm sorry, sir, but we only have cod or skate,' said the fishmonger.

'I don't want cod or skate. I want plaice,' repeated the customer, several times.

This infuriated the fishmonger, who asked the customer, 'If

you take the C out of cod you get "od". If you take the S out of skate you get "kate". What do you get if you take the "Flip" out of plaice?'

The customer thought for a moment, then replied, 'But there *is* no "flip" in plaice.'

'That's what I've been trying to tell you,' said the fishmonger.

T

for Travel

An Englishman, a Welshman and an Irishman are walking down the Strand and see a sign in the travel agent's window: 'FLORIDA – Return trip, only £25.' They say, 'This is cheap, let's try it.'

The next day they are rowing across the Atlantic. The Englishman says, 'Don't think much of this for a holiday.'

The Welshman says, 'I don't suppose it will be too bad; I expect they will fly us back.'

'They didn't last year,' says the Irishman.

A man found himself sitting next to a very glamorous blonde on an aeroplane. They were getting on very well, and he soon began to drop hints about making a date when they arrived at their destination. The blonde demurred, and said that the trouble was that she only liked making love to cowboys or Jews.

'Anyway,' she said, 'I don't even know your name. What is it?'

The man thought for a second then replied: 'Hopalong Goldberg.'

A man was registering at the reception desk of a rather grotty hotel. As he was given the key to his room the receptionist asked him, 'Have you got a good memory for faces, sir?'

'Yes, not bad. But why do you ask?'

'Because there's no shaving mirror in your room, sir.'

Bus Conductress: 'How old are you?'
Boy: 'Twelve.'
Bus Conductress: 'Well you shouldn't be smoking. Do you want to get me into trouble?'
Boy: 'I might. What time do you finish?'

A lady travelling by British Rail asked the guard to try and hurry up the train, which was running very, very late.

'It's urgent. I'm going to have a baby,' she told him.

'Madam, you should never have travelled in that condition.'

'When I got on the train,' she replied, 'I was not in this condition.'

A woman was driving up the M1 doing 70 mph in the centre lane. She was knitting at the same time, with her hands between the spokes of the steering wheel. A police car overtook her in the outside lane with all its lights flashing. As it drew level with her, a policeman unwound his window and shouted out to her, 'Pull over!'

'No,' she shouted back. 'Pair of socks!'

An Englishman was in trouble at Sydney Airport when he landed in Australia for the first time. The immigration official was pressing lots of buttons on a computer and examining his passport carefully on every page. Finally, after about five minutes, the official looked up and asked, 'Have you got a criminal record?'

'No,' the Englishman replied, 'I'm afraid not. I didn't know it was still necessary.'

The publicity office of a seaside town boasted that the resort was so clean that the gulls flew upside down.

An elderly lady had been told by her doctor to go away and recuperate after a severe operation. So she booked into a small hotel in the German mountains, where she would get peace and quiet. She wrote to the manager to check where the WC was, as she did not want it too far from her room. The German manager did not know what WC stood for. So he went to check with the local schoolmaster, who spoke good English.

'WC,' said the schoolmaster. 'That's easy. It's short for Wesleyan Chapel.'

So the manager, with the help of the schoolmaster, wrote back to the lady:

Dear Madam,
    In answer to your question, the WC is situated seven miles away in the middle of a forest, amid lovely surroundings. It's open on Sundays, Thursdays, and Fridays. This is unfortunate if you are in the habit of going regularly. But a number of people take their lunch with them and make a day of it. Others, who cannot spare the time, go by car and arrive at the last moment, as they are in a great hurry and cannot wait.
    The accommodation is good and there are twenty seats. But, should you be late, there is plenty of standing room. I would advise you to pay a visit on Thursday, when there is an organ accompaniment. The acoustics are excellent, even the most delicate sounds can be heard.
    I shall be delighted to accompany you and show you round, and if you wish will reserve a special seat for you.
                                        Your faithfully,

A man standing behind a young woman on a moving staircase at Piccadilly Circus tube station noticed that one of her breasts was hanging out of her dress. She didn't seem aware of it, so he bravely touched her on the shoulder and told her about it.

'Oh, thank goodness you've told me,' she said. 'I must have left the baby on the train.'

An enormously fat lady got on to a bus which was full, with standing room only. As she hung onto a strap she glared round the bus at the passengers, most of whom were men.

'Isn't anyone going to offer me a seat?'

At this, a tiny man got up and said meekly, 'I'm willing to make a small contribution.'

'Your car doesn't look so good. Have an accident?'

'No thanks. I've just had one.'

Motoring is like Russian roulette – you never know which driver is loaded.

In the early days people were flabbergasted when somebody drove at 15 mph: they still are.

The beauty of the old-fashioned blacksmith was that when you brought him your horses to be shod he didn't think of forty other things to be done to it.

Nothing depreciates a car faster than a neighbour buying a new one.

The greatest hazards on the road are those under 21 driving over 65 and those over 65 driving under 21.

Most road accidents are easily explained: the car is in gear and the driver's attention is in neutral.

Lady on bus: 'Do you stop at the Ritz, conductor?'

Conductor: 'No, madam. Not on my wages.'

A man was motoring along a main road when he saw a very attractive brunette by the side of the road, thumbing a lift. So he stopped and asked her to get into his car. As they were going along, in order to make conversation he asked her what she did for a living.

'Oh, I'm a witch,' she replied casually.

The motorist was naturally very surprised.

'I don't believe it,' he said. 'Can you prove it?'

Saying nothing the woman put her hand on his knee and then started to run her fingers up the inside of his thigh – and he immediately turned into a lay-by.

Lady on a Middle East cruise: 'Steward, can you please tell me where the nearest toilet is?'

Steward: 'Yes, madam. Port side.'

Lady: 'Good gracious. I can't possibly last that long.'

A man was belting up the road at 80 mph when just ahead of him a tractor with two men on it slowly came out of a gate and on to the road. Realising that if he went straight on he would hit the tractor, he swung violently to the left and shot through the gate into the field from which the tractor had just come. He bumped along the field parallel to the road for a few yards and then noticed a gap in the hedge. So he drove through it back on to the road and continued his journey at speed as if nothing had happened.

'You know, George,' said one of the men on the tractor to the other, 'we only just got out of that field in time.'

A motorist got lost on the A3 just after leaving Guildford. He stopped and addressed a man waiting at a bus stop.

'Excuse me, do you know the Hog's Back?'

'No,' replied the man. 'I didn't know that he'd been away.'

A Mini broke down and its owner was standing disconsolately by the side of the road. A very posh new Jaguar drew up and its driver asked if he could help.

The Mini owner said he did not know what was wrong, so the man in the Jaguar said, 'Okay, I'll give you a tow. I've got a very thin nylon rope in my boot. I'll go along slowly, but if there's anything wrong, blow your horn like mad.'

So they set off slowly and were cruising along at a steady 30 mph. Suddenly a big red Mercedes passed them at great speed. This nettled the Jaguar driver, who thought that, for the sake of Queen and country, he should show that British was the best. So, forgetting he had the Mini in tow, he set off in pursuit. He soon reached 100 mph and was gaining on the Mercedes. The poor man in the Mini wondered what on earth was happening. Remembering what he had been told he started to hoot like mad as his Mini was swaying and jumping about all over the place.

As he did so they passed a police car in a lay-by. The police patrolman, in amazement, got on the radio to speak to a colleague further up the road.

'There's a crazy race going on. A Mercedes going about 100 mph is just about to be passed by a Jaguar. And, believe it or not, right up behind the Jaguar, nearly touching his rear bumper, is a Mini. The Mini driver is hooting furiously and trying to pass them both.'

A man was travelling in the bottom berth of a second-class sleeper on the Glasgow to London night train. The top berth was unoccupied. After the train had stopped at Carlisle, the steward knocked on his door.

'Excuse me, sir, sorry to wake you. But I have a young lady here who cannot find a seat or a sleeping berth. Would you object if she used the top bunk? Otherwise she will have to stand up all the night.'

'Certainly, she can come in,' said the man sleepily.

He looked up to see a smashing blonde, who clambered up

to the top bunk and, after a few words of gratitude, appeared to settle down for the night.

But after a quarter of an hour or so she put her head over the edge and whispered, 'Are you awake? If so, I'm absolutely freezing up here. Could you go and ask the steward for another blanket, please?'

After a pause the man replied, 'I've got a far better idea. For the rest of the journey, why don't we pretend that we are a married couple?'

'Oh, yes,' said the blonde, 'that would be nice,' and swung her legs over the top bunk.

'Right,' said the man. 'Let's start as we're going to continue. *You* go and fetch the bloody blanket.'

A man was travelling in a very crowded bus. A young woman got on and whispered to him, 'Can I please have your seat? You see, I'm expecting.'

The man jumped up and said, 'Certainly, madam, but you don't *look* pregnant.'

'Well, I've only been pregnant for about half an hour,' she replied. 'But goodness, doesn't it make your back ache?'

U

for Umpires

W.G. Grace was batting on a very windy day, and a fast bowler succeeded in getting one past him which just flicked the bails off. The Doctor stood his ground and said to the umpire, 'Windy day today, umpire.'

Whereupon the umpire replied, 'Very windy indeed, Doctor – mind it doesn't blow your cap off on the way back to the pavilion!'

When Frank Tyson was a young man he once went in to bat against a team of first-class cricketers. His form was not very good. He missed the first ball, the next hit him on the pad, he snicked the third, and was clean bowled by the fourth. As he passed him, the umpire said to him, 'Aye lad, tha was lucky to make nought!'

A certain cricketer was a *very slow bowler* and had been hit more or less out of sight when at length the batsman missed a ball which pitched straight – like the others it was devoid of spin – and struck him on the pad. The bowler turned round with a howl of triumph to the umpire and cried 'How's that?'

'Not out,' said the umpire. The bowler was a very well-bred cricketer and it was not until the end of the over, when he had been hit for three more sixes, that he said to the umpire: 'That one pitched straight, didn't it?'

'Yes.'

'It didn't turn, did it?'

'No.'

'He didn't touch, did he?'

'No.'

'Then why wasn't he out?'

'It wasn't going fast enough to disturb the bails!'

Godfrey Evans made a particularly good stumping on the leg-side when playing in an up-country match on one of his tours of Australia. As he whipped off the bails he shouted to the umpire, 'How's that?' and the umpire replied, 'Bloody marvellous!'

Bill Reeves, the famous umpire, was seldom at a loss for a reply. But he was struck dumb on one occasion, as follows:

Surrey were playing for Gloucester at Cheltenham, and Alf Gover, Surrey's traditional number eleven, strode to the crease. He took up his stance ready to withstand the onslaught, scorning to take guard. Bill Reeves was never surprised at anything, but noting this somewhat irregular behaviour on Gover's part said, 'Hey, Alf, don't you want your guard?'

'No thanks,' said Alf, 'I've played here before.'

When he was at school, Gilbert Harding hated cricket. The headmaster, appreciating this, excused him playing on condition that he took some other exercise such as walking or tennis. But the games master was always very annoyed about this and got his own back one day (so he thought) by making Gilbert Harding umpire in the annual match of the Masters *v.* the Boys. The Masters batted first and the games master, resplendent in his Oxford Authentic cap, batted superbly and was 99 not out when a bowler from the end at which Gilbert Harding was umpiring hit the master high up on the left thigh. 'How's that?' said the bowler.

'Out,' said Gilbert. The games master was furious and as he

passed Gilbert on his way back to the pavilion said, 'Harding, you weren't paying attention. I wasn't out.'

Gilbert replied, 'On the contrary, sir, I *was* paying attention and you weren't out!'

In a Middlesex match at Lord's before the war, R.W.V. Robins had just completed a very productive over as far as the batsmen were concerned, and decided that it was time to make a change. He called over to Jim Smith, the Middlesex fast bowler, 'Take the next over at this end, Jim.'

Umpire Bill Reeves walked across to Robins and said, 'Do you want your sweater, sir?' As it was a hot day and Robins was perspiring, he rather grumpily said to Reeves: 'Keep the b***** sweater, and you know what you can do with it.'

'What, sir?' said Reeves, 'swords and all?'

Another story about Bill Reeves.

A young amateur playing for the first time for Lancashire was the most immaculate thing ever seen outside Savile Row. New pads, glistening white shirt and flannels, gaudy club cap. As he went in to bat it started to drizzle. At first ball there was an appeal for lbw against him. 'Out,' says Reeves.

During lunch the young amateur went up to Reeves, and said, 'I don't think I was out, Mr Reeves.'

'No, you weren't,' said Reeves and walked off. The young man fretted all the rest of the day and at close of play went up to Reeves again. 'Mr Reeves, excuse me, but I've been thinking about what you said at lunchtime. If you think I wasn't out, why on earth did you give me out?'

'Well, sonny, I was thinking of your poor old mother – whatever would she have done if you had caught your death of cold?'

In a village match a visiting batsman was hit high on the chest by the local fast bowler, the village blacksmith.

To his surprise the bowler appealed for lbw, and to his even greater surprise the umpire gave him out. As he passed the umpire on his way back to the pavilion, the batsman said, 'I couldn't possibly have been out, it hit me in the chest.'

'Well,' said the umpire, 'you look in the local *Gazette* next Thursday, and you'll see you were out right enough.'

'*You* look,' snorted the batsman. 'I'm the Editor!'

The game: Middlesex *v.* Hampshire at Lord's. The umpire: Bill Reeves, former Essex player. Middlesex batting, with H.J. Enthoven the non-striker, and Jack Newman bowling for Hampshire. The striker played the ball towards mid-on and called for a run; but the bowler, running across to the ball, inadvertently impeded Enthoven, who fell and was out of his ground when the bowler's wicket was broken. Reeves, however, gave him not out, on the grounds that he had been balked by the bowler. Tennyson, the Hampshire captain, reported the matter and, after a week, Reeves was called before the MCC Committee.

Lord Hawke, in the chair, called upon Reeves to describe the incident in his own words. Having done so, he waited nervously for the Committee's decision; but after what seemed to be an interminable interval, he could no longer contain himself and burst out, 'Well, my Lord, what would *you* have done if you had been the umpire?'

Lord Hawke, taken aback, replied, 'Well, I don't know, I don't know.'

To which Reeves replied, 'A damned fine umpire *you'd* make, my Lord. You've had a week to think about it; I only had a second!'

The story went that Lord Hawke burst out laughing and that Reeves got away with a caution.

A village umpire gave a batsman out lbw. 'But I can't be out,' said the batsman as he saw the umpire's finger raised in the air. 'I hit the ball.'

The umpire thought for a second and then said, 'Yes, I know you did. I'm signalling a bye.'

Surrey were playing Middlesex at the Oval and Bill Reeves was one of the umpires. Nigel Haig opened the bowling and as usual Sandham went in first for Surrey. As you know, he was not very tall and a ball from Haig hit him in the navel and there was a loud appeal.

'Not out,' called Reeves.

'Why not?' asked Haig.

'Too high,' said Reeves.

Haig went back to his mark muttering, possibly thinking that even if a ball hit a little chap like Sandham on the head, it couldn't be too high. A few balls later a beautiful ball beat Sandham all ends up and hit him on the pads.

'What about that one, then?' yelled Haig.

'Not out,' said Reeves.

'Why not?' asked Haig.

'Too low!' said Reeves – and that ended all arguments for that day!

During a village match the umpire was heckled by supporters of the home side. After a while he left the field and went and sat down in a deckchair among the noisy spectators. 'What's the idea?' he was asked.

'It appears you get the best view from here,' he replied.

A batsman was given out lbw and strongly disagreed with the umpire's decision. However, he restrained himself until the next interval when he went up to a man in a white coat and said, 'Umpire, I wasn't out; you need your eyes tested!'

'Oh, I do, do I?' said the man. 'Well you'd better have yours tested too. I'm selling ice cream!'

V

for VIPs

A few years ago the Pope paid one of his official visits to Ireland. As his plane approached Dublin, because of strong cross-winds, it was diverted to Shannon. Waiting on the tarmac at Dublin was a glistening white Rolls-Royce, in which the driver, Michael Murphy was to drive the Pope to where he was staying.

The airport authorities immediately instructed Michael to drive as fast as he could to meet the Pope at Shannon Airport. He drove there in time to see the Pope come down the steps of his plane, and bend down and kiss the Irish soil as was his custom. The Pope then looked up and saw the glistening white Rolls-Royce. His eyes gleamed and he went across to the car, alongside which Michael was standing, waiting.

'What's your name?' asked the Pope.

'Michael Murphy, your Holiness.'

'Well, Michael, you go and sit in the back seat. I'm going to drive.'

So they set off with the Pope driving at great speed along the narrow Irish roads. He was soon going at 90 mph, and shortly afterwards he was passed and flagged down by a police car with all its lights flashing.

The policeman approached the Pope and asked him for his driving licence. The Pope, who always kept it in his vestments, handed the licence to the policeman, who thanked him politely.

After he had taken down all the details, the policeman withdrew out of the Pope's hearing and rang his superintendent on his mobile phone.

'We've got trouble here, superintendent,' he said. 'I've just stopped a VIP's car going at 90 mph.'

'How important is he?' asked the superintendent. 'Is he as important as Terry Wogan, or the Prime Minister or even Royalty? Anyhow, what's his name?'

'I don't know who he is, sir,' said the policeman. 'But he must be very important. He's being driven by the Pope.'

General de Gaulle was asked if he would like a state funeral when he died. 'No,' he said. 'It would be a waste of money. I shall only be gone for three days.'

The late **Duke of Norfolk** used to tell a story about his trainer, called Sid Fidell. He was in the habit of writing long reports to the Duke after each race, even though they always met every Friday at Arundel. The Duke suggested to him that a short telegram after each race would suffice, and that they could go into more details when they met on the Fridays.

Next week the Duke had a horse running on Tuesday afternoon and was puzzled to receive the following telegram that evening: SF-SF-SF-SF.

He assumed it was from Sid, but couldn't make head or tail of it. So when they met on the Friday the Duke asked Sid what on earth it meant.

'Quite easy, Your Grace. It described what happened to your horse last Tuesday:

*S*tarted *F*arted – *S*lipped and *F*ell

*S*ee you *F*riday *S*id *F*idell.'

Mrs Gandhi was on a state visit to Singapore and was watching a military parade with the prime minister, Lee Kwan Yew. They were sitting under a canopy when suddenly the skies darkened and down came a tropical storm. The parade ground was soon flooded and the rain was so heavy that it came through the canopy under which Mrs Gandhi was sitting. She got drenched. Remarkably the Prime Minister was lucky, and his bit of the canopy did not leak. He was quite dry. He apologised profusely to Mrs Gandhi that she was sopping wet.

'Thank you,' she said, as attendants rushed forward to try to dry her, 'but I still don't understand why it didn't Lee Kwan Yew.'

The well-known architect **Sir Edward Maufe** arrived late at the reception before a very formal dinner. The toastmaster had given up announcing the guests. So Sir Edward, not wishing to cause any fuss, sidled up to his hostess and murmured his name.

'I'm Maufe,' he said.

'Oh, really,' the hostess replied. 'I'm so sorry you can't stop for the dinner.'

Lord Birkenhead was once buttonholed by a long-winded bore who insisted on recounting at great length the poor treatment which he had received at a certain hotel.

'But, of course,' he concluded, 'as soon as they knew who I was, everything was all right.'

'And *who* were you?' Lord Birkenhead asked politely.

George Bernard Shaw was once leaving a party.

'Well, Mr Shaw, I hope you enjoyed yourself,' said his hostess.

'Yes, thank you, madam, I did. I was the only thing there was to enjoy.'

A glamorous lady once approached the portrait painter, the late **Edward Halliday**, and asked him if he would paint her in the nude.

'Yes, I will,' he said after a bit of thought. 'But on one condition. I must keep my socks on. I have to have somewhere to stick my brushes.'

George Bernard Shaw and **Winston Churchill** did not get on too well. In the thirties, when Churchill was in the political wilderness, Shaw sent him four tickets for the first night of one of his new plays, adding: 'These are for you and your friends – if you have any.'

Churchill returned the tickets saying he was already engaged on that evening. 'But, I would very much like to have tickets for the second night – if there is one.'

When **William Douglas-Home** was at Eton he was asked to write as briefly as possible on either: (1) The Future of Socialism, or (2) The Future of Coal. He chose the second question and wrote just one word: 'Smoke'.

Field-Marshall Lord Montgomery was inspecting a parade of war veterans. He came to a man with only one arm, his other sleeve hanging down empty.

'Where did you get that?' asked Monty.

'Fighting for the 8th Army at the Battle of Alamein, sir,' replied the veteran.

Further up the line was another veteran, also with one empty sleeve.

'And where did you get that?' asked Monty again.

'Fighting for the 8th Army in Sicily, sir,' was the reply.

Each time Monty uttered words of sympathy and encouragement, and recalled the glorious exploits of the 8th Army. Right at the end of the line was a man with no hands showing out of either sleeve.

'Where did you get that?' asked Monty yet again.

'At Burton's, sir. It's going back tomorrow. The sleeves are far too long.'

During the American Civil War **General Sedgemore** was inspecting his front line. He was a brave man and ignored warnings from his junior officers not to put his head over the parapet to see the enemy's positions.

'It's quite safe,' he said, as he stuck his head over the top. 'They couldn't hit an elephant at this dis . . .'

Lord Reith, the first Director General of the BBC, was famous for his puritanical outlook. He required and demanded the highest moral standards from his staff. Woe betide any defaulter. Even the chief engineer was sacked because he told Reith that he was being divorced by his wife. One evening Reith was going round the studios in Broadcasting House and went unexpectedly into one of the drama studios. There, to his horror, was a well-known producer making love to one of the leading actresses in the BBC Repertory *on the table* in the studio.

Reith closed the door quietly and, rushing back to his office, summoned one of his assistants.

'I want you to get rid of the drama producer John Smith and the actress Betty Jones. I have found them making love on a studio table.'

His assistant began to stammer and demur.

'Don't argue,' thundered Reith. 'Get rid of them both *immediately*.'

'But, sir,' said the assistant, 'Smith is far and away our best drama producer and Jones our best actress. Furthermore, the play they are rehearsing is already billed in *Radio Times* and goes out next week. It would create an awful scandal if it was cancelled now. The reason would be bound to come out.'

Reith thought for a moment and then made his decision. 'Very well, then. Get rid of the table.'

On Ted Dexter's MCC tour of Australia the manager was the late **Duke of Norfolk**. It was a surprising choice. Dukes are not usually managers of cricket teams. But he was very popular in Australia. They called him Dukey and he endeared himself to them by leasing a racehorse wherever the MCC were playing. When they were playing against South Australia at Adelaide the duke had a horse running at a small country racecourse called Gawlor not far from Adelaide. He went to see it run and walked down to the paddock to talk to the trainer before the race. The horse was in a far corner under a gum tree, and as the duke strolled across the paddock he saw the trainer take something out of his pocket and give it to the horse to eat. The duke, remembering his position as a member of the Jockey Club and the Queen's representative at Ascot, was worried about dope.

'What's that you've just given the horse to eat?' he asked the trainer anxiously.

'Oh, Your Grace,' replied the trainer, looking rather guilty. 'It was just a lump of sugar. In fact I'm going to have one myself. Would you like one too, Your Grace?'

As he spoke the trainer took a lump of sugar out of his pocket and ate it. He then offered another one to the duke who, very much relieved, thought he ought to humour the trainer and took the lump of sugar and put it in his mouth. He then chatted to the trainer and finally began to walk back to the stands. Five minutes before the race the jockeys came into the paddock and the duke's jockey went up to the trainer under the gum tree for his riding instructions.

The trainer told him, 'Listen. This is a seven-furlong race. For the first five furlongs keep him on the bit and keep him tucked in behind the others. Then for the last two furlongs let him go and give him all you've got. If anyone passes you after that it's either myself or the Duke of Norfolk.'

Someone once wrote an article about the late Sir Francis Chichester. There was an accompanying picture under which the caption read: *Sir Francis Chichester – the great yachtsman who, with his 24-foot cutter, circumcised the world.*

The veteran actor A.E. Matthews, who went on acting well into his eighties, used to say, 'I am so old that in the morning my wife brings me a cup of tea and a copy of *The Times*. I drink the tea, then look at the obituary column in *The Times*. If I'm not in it, I get up.'

In the early thirties **King Abdulla of Jordan** was the guest of King George V and Queen Mary at a banquet in Buckingham Palace. When the meal started, a royal flunkey brought an enormous tureen of soup to the top table. He helped Queen Mary and was about to give some to King Abdulla when the latter said loudly, 'No thank you. No soup for me. It makes me fart.'

There was consternation among the royal guests, until King Abdulla went on, patting his enormous stomach: 'Look,' he said. 'I am fart enough already.'

W

for Wedlock

A wife was a bit worried about her sex life with her husband, so bought him a book on sex for Christmas. In the New Year she asked him if he had picked up any tips which would help make their sex together more satisfactory.

'Yes,' he said. 'There was an article which said how much it helped if the woman moaned during the climax of the act. Let's try it tonight.'

So, when things were going well later that night, his wife whispered, 'Is this the moment? Shall I start to moan now?'

'Yes,' he replied in a husky voice. 'Start now.'

'Right,' said the wife. 'Why on earth do you always leave me to do all the washing up?'

A mother of eight young children was sitting stitching up her husband's pyjamas when a friend came in and asked her why she was doing it.

'A stitch in time saves nine,' was the reply.

A young man went to ask his girlfriend's father whether he could marry her.

'Certainly, dear boy. Of course you can. I'm delighted. But, I think I should warn you that she's got acute angina.'

'You're telling me, sir,' replied the young man.

A young man was very nervous before the first night of his

honeymoon. He had never made love before and confided his worry to his best friend who was already married.

'Don't worry,' said the friend. 'Once in bed you'll soon find out what's what.'

So on the first night the bridegroom lay alongside his bride and started to stroke her body. After a bit he asked her, 'What's that?'

'What's what?' she said.

'Ah,' he sighed with relief. 'That's it.'

A businessman missed his last train and had to take the milk train which got him home about 4 a.m. All the lights were on in the house and when he opened the front door his wife was standing in the hall, obviously very distressed.

'Oh, thank God you've come home at last, darling,' she said. 'We've had a burglar in our bedroom.'

'Did he get anything?' asked the husband anxiously.

'Yes,' she said, 'that's the trouble. He did, I thought it was you!'

A duke and his duchess were arguing about money – or the lack of it.

'We've simply got to economise somehow,' said the duke. 'If only you could cook properly, we could sack the cook.'

'In that case,' said the duchess, 'if only you could make love properly, we could also sack the chauffeur.'

'For twenty years my husband and I were very happy.'

'What happened then?'

'We met.'

A married couple had ten children in the first twelve years of their marriage. The trouble was that the wife was stone deaf and whenever her husband said, 'Shall we go to sleep or what?' she always said, 'What?'

A man dreaded his mother-in-law coming to stay. She was such a know-all. Whatever he said, she would say, 'I know, I know.'

He might have heard the late news on the TV, or read a headline in the paper. No matter what it was, if he mentioned it, back came the reply, 'I know, I know.'

When he learnt from his wife that her mother was coming to stay for Christmas, he had an idea. One morning he went out to the milkman who had just driven up in his milk cart.

'Will you hire me your horse for Christmas morning? I will pay you anything reasonable. I shall only need him for about an hour before breakfast on Christmas Day.'

The milkman agreed terms and early on Christmas morning made the man's house his last call. He and the man unharnessed the horse and the man asked the milkman if he would help him take the horse inside the house, then take him upstairs and finally put him in the bath. After a great struggle they achieved this, damaging a lot of paintwork up the stairs. But they managed it without waking anyone in the house. When they got downstairs, the man gave the milkman a cup of tea. The latter was naturally a bit perplexed.

'Why on earth do you want to put a horse in the bath?' asked the milkman.

'Well, it's like this,' said the man. 'My mother-in-law is staying with us. Whatever I say she always answers with: "I know, I know." So when she gets up this morning she will go to the bathroom and she will scream and come rushing out, shouting, "Help, help! There's a horse in the bath," and I shall say, casually: "I know, I know." '

A young man and his fiancée were taking a walk in the woods. They sat down under a tree and after a short while the inevitable happened. Afterwards the young woman cried bitterly.

'Oh, I feel such a sinner doing it before we are married. I don't know how I can face my parents after being so wicked twice in an afternoon.'

'Twice?' said the young man. 'We only did it once.'

'O, but you *are* going to do it again, aren't you?' she said.

A woman was asking a friend how her marriage was going and whether she was happy with her husband.

'I don't know what to say, dear,' said her friend. 'Bert works very hard at his garage and I think he's doing too much. The job is getting on top of him. The other night in bed I woke up and found he was stroking my bottom and saying, "Disgraceful. Only five thousand miles and the tread has gone already." '

A boy told his father that he wanted to get married.

'Very well, son. Whom do you want to marry?'

'Miss Green, Dad.'

'You can't marry her. She's your half-sister. When I was a lad, I had a bike and used to get around a bit.'

'All right, then, Dad. I'll marry Miss White.'

'You can't do that either. She's also your half-sister.'

The boy was very despondent and told his mum that his dad said he couldn't marry Miss Green or Miss White as they were his half-sisters.

'You go and marry which of them you like,' said his mum. 'He's not your father anyway.'

A man came home completely unexpectedly and found a naked man talking to his wife on the sofa. He was furious.

'What's he doing here?'

'It's all right, darling. It's a nudist who has come in to use the phone.'

Two young wives were discussing the sexual prowess of their respective husbands. One of them complained that hers was not too good.

'Oh,' said the other, 'mine was the same a year ago. But I made him take some rhino-horn pills and ever since then his performance has been magnificent.'

Her friend thanked her and said she would get her husband to take the pills also. They met a month or two later and the friend who had suggested the pills asked how they had worked.

'Oh, absolutely marvellously. He has become an insatiable lover. But I do have one worry. When we're out walking, every time he sees a Land Rover he tries to charge it.'

'Here's a letter from my wife.'
    'But there's nothing written on it.'
    'No. We're not on speaking terms.'

'I call my wife Radio 4.'
    'Why?'
    'Because she never has anything on after midnight.'

A woman went to a medium to get in touch with her late husband. After a few sessions she was at last successful.

'How are you, darling?' she asked. 'What are you doing?'

'I'm having a wonderful time,' came back the voice. 'I sleep late in the morning. Have a little sex when I wake up, then go for a short walk to get some food. Then back home for more sex and sleep, and so it goes on every twenty-four hours.'

His wife was naturally a bit shocked. 'But what are you? Have you been reincarnated?'

'Yes, I have. I'm a rabbit on Wimbledon Common.'

A wife asked her husband if he would remarry if she were to die. The husband hesitated and then said, 'No, darling. The thought has never entered my head. I can't think of anyone whom I would want to live with.'

'But,' persisted the wife, 'just supposing you *did* remarry, would you give her my jewels?'

'I suppose I might,' conceded her husband.

'And what about my golf clubs?' asked the wife.

'Oh no, there'd be no point in doing that,' he replied. 'She's left-handed.'

'Where are you going?'

'I'm going to fetch the doctor. I don't like the look of my wife.'

'I'll come with you. I hate the sight of mine.'

'My wife's just left me.'

'Oh, really. How much?'

'Where's your wife these days?'

'She's gone to the West Indies.'

'Jamaica?'

'No. She went of her own accord.'

'My wife's in hospital.'

'Flu?'

'Yes – and crashed.'

'My love for my wife is like a kangaroo with rheumatism – it knows no bounds.'

An artist was embracing his attractive young model. Suddenly he heard his wife coming up the stairs. 'Quick,' he said, 'take your clothes off immediately, I'm meant to be painting you.'

'They're a fastidious couple – she's fast, and he's hideous.'

An elderly couple decided to celebrate their diamond wedding by having a second honeymoon. They went to the same town, same hotel, same bedroom, same bed. When they went to bed, the wife put her arms round him and said, 'Darling, do you remember how romantic you were sixty years ago? You bit me in the neck, you bit me in the shoulder and then you bit me in the breast.'

The husband leapt out of bed and went to the bathroom.

'What are you doing?' the wife replied.

'Getting my teeth!' he replied.

A young, recently married man was a member of his local Round Table. Once a month they had a meeting when the newer members had to address the other members on a subject which was drawn out of a hat. He drew out 'sex', and proceeded to give a masterly discourse on the subject based on his new experiences as a married man. When he got home he told his wife that he had had to make a speech, but was too bashful to say what the subject was. So when she asked him, he said, 'Oh, er . . . yachting.'

The next day the young wife went into her bank and the manager came forward and said how excellent her husband had been, with such an expert knowledge of his subject.

'That's funny,' she said. 'He's only done it twice. The first time he was sick. The second time his hat flew off.'

X

for Crosstalk

'What do your mother and father do?'
  'Oh, they're in the iron and steel business. My mother irons, my father steals.'

'I call my dog Isaiah.'
  'Isaiah? Why that?'
  'Because one eye's 'igher than the other.'

'I call my dog Corsets.'
  'Why?'
  'Because he's tied up all day but let out at night.'

'I've just bought a goat.'
  'Oh really? Where does he sleep?'
  'Under my bed.'
  'But what about the smell?'
  'Oh, he'll soon get used to that!'

'Every day my dog and I go for a tramp in the woods.'
  'Does the dog enjoy it?'
  'Yes *he* does. But the tramp is getting a bit fed up.'

'Every time the bell rings my dog goes into a corner.'
   'Why's that?'
   'Oh, he's a boxer.'

'I've just saved a girl from drowning.'
   'How did it happen?'
   'Well, I was walking along the beach when I saw a girl slowly drifting out to sea.'
   'So you jumped in after her?'
   'No, I threw her a cake of soap.'
   'Whatever for?'
   'To wash her back, of course.'

'I've just been up to Scotland on holiday. All the Scotsmen were wearing kilts.'
   'Really? Did you see the Trossachs?'
   'No. It wasn't windy.'

'My small nephew has got three feet.'
   'Really? That's extraordinary. Has he always had them?'
   'No. I got a letter from my sister this morning which said that I wouldn't recognise little Johnny now. He's grown another foot.'

'My mother hasn't been kissed by my father for ten years.'
   'Why not?'
   'She won't let him kiss her when he's drunk, and when he's sober he doesn't want to.'

'What's the difference between a woman in a short skirt getting out of a car and a rude joke?'
   'I don't know. What *is* the difference?'
   'Sometimes you see it, sometimes you don't.'

'I come of an old musical family. You know the great Handel?'
'Yes.'
'Well my father used to turn it.'

(Very fast)
'You're looking very smart. Where do you get your ties?'
  'Thailand.'
'And your collars?'
  'Colorado.'
'Your vests?'
  'Vestminster.'
'Your pants?'
  'Pannsylvania.'
'Your socks?'
  'Sauchiehall Street.'
'Your shoes?'
  'Sherusalem.'
'And your shirt. Where does that come from?'
  'From the Isle of Man.'
'How do you know?'
  'Because it hasn't got a tail.'

'What did you have for breakfast?'
  'Haddock.'
  'Finnan?'
  'No. Thick'un.'

'If I post this letter tonight, will it get to Brighton in two days' time?'
  'Well it might do – even in these days.'
  'I bet you it won't.'
  'Why not?'
  'It's addressed to Southampton.'

108

'What's your uncle doing these days?'
  'Oh, he's in low water.'
  'Oh, I'm sorry.'
  'No, not to worry. He gives swimming lessons. He's a con-
tortionist – he can swim with one foot on the bottom.'

'My son is an electrician and I don't like it.'
  'Why?'
  'Well, he's always wiring for money.'

'My Uncle George has barometeritis.'
  'Why?'
  'The glass keeps going up and down.'

'I've just seen forty men under one umbrella and not one
of them has got wet.'
  'It must have been a very large umbrella!'
  'No. It wasn't raining.'

'It's all in the papers tonight.'
  'What is?'
  'Fish and chips.'

'I know a place where women only wear necklaces.'
  'Where on earth is that?'
  'Round the neck.'

'Who's that girl I saw you with the other day?'
  'It was a girl from the school.'
  'Teacher?'
  'No. It wasn't necessary.'

'Where are you taking that basket of plums?'
    'I'm taking them to Buckingham Palace for the Queen.'
    'Why?'
    'Because in "God Save the Queen" it says, "Send her Victorias".'

Y

for Young people's jokes

'Shall I tell you the story of the pencil?'
   'No. There's no point in it.'

Q: What do Eskimos call their money?
A: Iced lolly.

Q: What did Adam do when he wanted some sugar?
A: He raised Cain.

Q: What do you call a cat who has swallowed a duck?
A: A duck-filled fatty puss.

Q: What was Dracula's favourite song?
A: Fangs for the memory.

Q: How do you communicate with a fish?
A: Drop him a line.

Q: Why are tall people always the laziest?
A: Because they lie longer in bed.

Q: Who invented the five-day week?
A: Robinson Crusoe, because he had all his work done by Friday.

Q: What always succeeds?
A: A budgie with no teeth.

Q: Why do white sheep eat more than black sheep?
A: Because there are more white sheep.

Q: Why are policemen so strong?
A: Because they can hold up all the traffic with one hand.

Q: What do you call an Arabian milk farmer?
A: A milk sheik.

'Do you know the secret story of the pat of butter?'
  'No.'
  'Well, I'd better not tell you. You'd only spread it.'

'Do you know the story of the dustcart?'
  'No.'
  'Well, I shouldn't worry. It's a load of rubbish.'

'Do you know the story of the bed?'
  'No.'
  'I can't tell you as I haven't made it up yet.'

Q: Why is it difficult to keep a secret at the North Pole?
A: Because your teeth tend to chatter.

Q: What did the skunk say when the wind changed direction?
A: 'Ah, it's all coming back to me now.'

Q: What do you get if you cross a crocodile with a rose?
A: I don't know, but I wouldn't try smelling it.

Q: Why do leopards never get far when they escape from the zoo?
A: Because they're always spotted.

Q: What did the bell say when it fell in the water?
A: 'I'm wringing wet.'

Q: What did Hamlet say when he went into a telephone box?
A: 2p or not 2p, that is the question.

Q: What did they do when the Forth Bridge collapsed?
A: Built a fifth.

Q: What sort of robbery is the easiest?
A: A safe robbery.

Q: What did the burglar say to the watchmaker?
A: 'Sorry to have taken so much of your valuable time.'

Q: What prize did the man who invented doorknockers win?
A: The Nobel Prize.

Q: What's the best thing to give as a parting gift?
A: A comb.

Q: What can go up a drainpipe down, but can't go down a drainpipe up?
A: An umbrella.

Q: What's the best cure for water on the brain?
A: A tap on the head.

'I won't tell you the story about the umbrella.'
  'Why not?'
  'Because it would be over your head . . .'

'What are you doing, Johnny?'
  'I'm writing a letter to my cousin Pat.'
  'Don't be silly. You can't write.'
  'It doesn't matter. Pat can't read.'

Old lady to small boy: 'And what might your name be, young man?'
Boy: 'It might be Cecil. But it ain't. It's William.'

'Willie, if you had £5 in one pocket of your trousers and £2 in the other, what would you have?'
  'Someone else's trousers on, Miss.'

'Dad, what are you going to do with that manure?'
  'Put it on my strawberries, son.'
  'That's funny. Mum always gives us sugar and cream.'

Q: What would happen to the economy if pigs could fly?
A: Bacon would go up.

Q: Who were the ice cream men in the Bible?
A: Walls of Jericho and Lyons of Judah.

Q: If a Frenchman is shot out of a cannon, what's his name?
A: Napoleon Blownapart.

Q: What's the shape of a kiss?
A: Elliptical.

Q: What do you call a deaf elephant?
A: Anything you like. He won't hear you.

Q: How do you get down off an elephant?
A: You don't. You get it off a swan.

Q: Why did the bees go on strike?
A: For shorter flowers and more money.

Q: What kind of lighting did Noah have in the Ark?
A: Flood lighting.

Q: Why don't barbers cut hair any longer?
A: Because they cut it shorter.

Q: What happened to the man who stole a calendar?
A: He got twelve months.

Q: What would Neptune say if the seas dried up?
A: I haven't a notion.

Q. What is the difference between Noah's Ark and Joan of Arc?
A: One was made of wood, the other was Maid of Orleans.

Q: What's the difference between an old Etonian and Jonah?
A: One was brought up at Eton, the other was eaten and brought up.

Q: What did the grasshopper say to God the day he was created?
A: Lord, you didn't half make me jump.

Q: How do you make a bandstand?
A: Take away their chairs.

Z

for Bends

A man was driving his large Bentley down a winding country lane. As he approached a sharp corner a lady in a Mini came slowly round and had to go up on to the grass verge to avoid the Bentley. She wound down her window and shouted out, 'Pig!'

The driver of the Bentley was annoyed at this and, unwinding *his* window, shouted back, 'Silly old bitch!'

He then drove slowly forward and, as he went round the corner, he saw a large pig squatting in the middle of the lane.

OVER THE LIMIT
My Secret Diaries

Bob Monkhouse

Bob's journals of the last few years are interwoven with memories of a life in comedy. There are meetings with remarkable comedians – some like Paul Merton at the height of their powers, others like Dick Emery and Benny Hill in sad decline – and Bob reflects on what makes comedians great. Above all here is a wealth of wonderful true adventures, star scandals and gossip about the famous and infamous personalities he's known intimately, with more stars than the most lavish Royal Variety Performance, including: Peter Sellers, Rex Harrison, Lew Dawson, Elton John, Larry Grayson, Bing Crosby, Beryl Reid, k d lang and Luciano Pavarotti. As Bob puts it, 'All the good stuff I couldn't put in my autobiography because there wouldn't have been room for me!' There has always been room for Bob in the hearts of the British public, and this very, very funny book is just one more reason why he so richly deserves his place in our affections.

Praise for Bob's memoirs:

'Hilarious... amazing' *Sunday People*

'Hugely entertaining... a scintillating treasure trove of shamelessly dropped names, risqué jokes, gossip and scandalous revelations' Val Hennessy, *Daily Mail*

'Riveting... packed with cracking true stories' Sun

'An entertaining and abrasive canter through his up-and-down life... Witty, moving, candid – and very well written' *Sunday Express*

'Winning... genuinely funny' *Sunday Times*